Table of Contents

Welcome to React Router Ready!

Hello, I'm Steven Spadotto. I've been a full-stack web developer for over 10 years. I've had the pleasure to work for great companies in the education, gaming, and e-commerce industries, where I helped architecture, design, and develop web applications. Over the years, I gained valuable experience working with in-demand front-end technologies such as JavaScript, TypeScript, Angular, and of course, React.

Throughout my career, I've had the pleasure to mentor several front-end developers. It has given me the opportunity to help them gain knowledge and experience with technologies such as React. It's a rewarding process where I get to see front-end developers get more comfortable and more confident with the tools they use.

I've also taught React courses for beginners. Students often asked me if I could point them to a dependable resource that they could refer back to for future reference. Their question motivated me to publish my first book, React Ready (https://lumin8media.com/books/react-ready-learn-modern-react-with-typescript). React Router Ready is the sequel to React Ready.

React Router is the most popular third-party library in the React ecosystem. This means that learning React Router is essential for React developers.

Throughout this book, we'll be building a React Router powered React web app. This book will take you from being a React Router rookie to becoming a skilled developer with React Router. If you want to build modern React web applications with Vite, React, React Router, and TypeScript, then this is the book for you.

React developers are highly sought after on the job market. I am confident that your skill set and your value on the job market will jump after you learn how to use React Router effectively.

Learning something new is never easy. Remember not to be hard on yourself. Learning takes time. Celebrate every section that you complete. If you get stuck and something isn't immediately clear for you, take a break and return to it later. Feel free to message me on Twitter (https://twitter.com/stevenspads). I would be happy to help with any topic that you are struggling with. Enjoy your learning journey, as you become React Router Ready!

Introduction

React Router is the most popular routing library for React. In React, routing is the process of navigating to different pages, or parts of pages. React Router is a routing library for React that supports both client and server-side routing.

React Router provides a declarative API for adding to and updating the user's navigation history to allow the user to navigate across a web app. When client-side routing is used, React Router turns our React app into a *SPA* (Single-Page Application) where routing is done without reloading the page.

If you're new to React, it may be shocking to find out that a router isn't part of the React library. React is simply focused on providing the building blocks required for creating dynamic user interfaces. The rest is left for third-party libraries, like React Router. React Router follows a similar structure as React. Under the hood of React Router is just a collection of React components and React Hooks.

This book dives into detail on how to use React Router to build a modern React app with TypeScript. The focus of this book is on the more popular client-side routing of React Router rather than the server-side routing capabilities. For server-side routing, using a framework like Next.js or Remix is a better option. Remix was actually created by the creators of React Router and it is based on React Router. Learning React Router will help you learn Remix.

A basic understanding of React will help you learn how to use React Router more effectively. If you haven't read React Ready yet, I'd suggest to start reading that book before continuing with this book.

This book will use React with TypeScript. A basic understanding of TypeScript is helpful for going through this book, but is not required.

At the time of this writing (July 2023), we will be using the latest version of React Router (version 6.14).

Setup

Let's go over some setup steps to make sure that your machine can clone, install, and run the sample app from the GitHub code repository included with this book.

System Setup

The React app that we will build in this book can be found in the following GitHub repository (https://github.com/stevenspads/react-router-ready). To run the app on your local computer, you'll need the following to be installed.

- Git (https://git-scm.com/downloads)

- Node.js (https://nodejs.org/en/download)

- npm (included with Node.js installation)

Run the following commands in your terminal to see if they are properly installed.

```
git --version
node --version
npm --version
```

GitHub repository

The React app for this book is an online store app that manages an inventory of products. We'll be able to create, view, edit, and delete products. The GitHub repository contains the completed app.

You'll need to clone the GitHub repository on your local machine to be able to run and inspect it locally. Enter the following commands in your command-line.

```
git clone https://github.com/stevenspads/react-router-ready
cd react-router-ready
# if you prefer using npm, run these commands:
npm install
npm run dev
# if you prefer using yarn, run these commands:
yarn
yarn dev
```

This will start a development server at http://127.0.0.1:5173, or http://localhost:5173. When the development server starts, this address will be displayed in VS

Code's terminal. Click on it to open it in your web browser. If you have another application running on port 5173, consider freeing up that port by stopping the application running on it.

The code in the GitHub repository is a React app scaffolded with Vite. Vite is a build tool that provides a fast and smooth development experience for building modern web apps. By default, Vite's development server runs on port 5173.

Vite

Vite (https://vitejs.dev) is a very performant front-end tool that gives us a development server to run our React application locally, and a *build* command that bundles our code, producing optimized static assets for production.

Vite supports modern front-end libraries such as React, Vue, Preact, and Svelte, and it has TypeScript support.

Visual Studio Code

Using Visual Studio Code (https://code.visualstudio.com) as your code editor will help speed up development because of its smart IntelliSense and great TypeScript support. We can get type definitions for variables just by hovering over them. I recommend downloading, installing, and using it if it isn't already your main code editor.

The sample app

You might be wondering how I created the sample app for this book. Let me guide you through each step I took. To create the sample application for this book, I followed the following steps. You can use them to create a new project of your own.

1. Create the app with Vite

Create a new Vite-powered React app with the following command: `yarn create vite`. The project creation process will ask you a few questions. Here are my answers to the Vite project setup questions.

- Project name: `react-router-ready`

- Select a framework: React

- Select a variant: TypeScript

2. Install React Router

Install React Router with the following command: `yarn add react-router-dom`.

3. Install Tailwind CSS

We will follow the official guide (https://tailwindcss.com/docs/guides/vite) to adding TailwindCSS to a Vite-powered React project.

1. Install TailwindCSS and its dependencies: `yarn add -D tailwindcss postcss autoprefixer`

2. Generate the required configuration files: `npx tailwindcss init -p`

3. Add the paths to all of your React files in your `tailwind.config.js` file. This configuration file should look like the following:

```
/** @type {import('tailwindcss').Config} */
export default {
  content: ["./index.html", "./src/**/*.{ts,tsx}"],
  theme: {
    extend: {},
  },
  plugins: [],
};
```

4. Add the `@tailwind` directives for each of Tailwind's layers to the project's `./src/index.css` file. The `index.css` file should look like the following:

```
@tailwind base;
@tailwind components;
@tailwind utilities;
```

4. Remove Vite demo code and files

- Delete the code in `/src/App.tsx` and delete the `/src/App.css` file.

- Delete the `/assets` folder and the `react.svg` in it.

- Delete `vite.svg` in the `/public` folder.

5. Set up Prettier

Prettier is a code formatter that enforces a consistent style by parsing the project code and re-printing it with its own rules that take things like the maximum line length into account, wrapping code when necessary. There's plenty of other code formatting rules that we can configure.

Every time a file is saved, we can configure Prettier to auto-format it for us. This will save lots of time during code reviews.

Run the following command to install Prettier: `yarn add -D prettier eslint-config-prettier`. Then, create a `.prettierrc.cjs` file with the following formatting rules.

```
module.exports = {
  trailingComma: "all",
  tabWidth: 2,
  useTabs: false,
  semi: true,
  singleQuote: true,
  printWidth: 120,
  bracketSpacing: true
};
```

Next, create a `.prettierignore` file to specify all the files that Prettier should ignore while formatting the project's files. Add the following lines to the file.

```
node_modules/
dist/
.prettierrc.cjs
```

In the `package.json` file, under the `scripts` section, add the following.

```
"format": "prettier --write \"src/**/*.ts(x)\""
```

Now, run `yarn format` to format all the TypeScript files within the project.

We can install the Prettier extension for VS Code to allow us to auto-format code when a file is saved. Click on the VS Code Extensions icon in the left sidebar. Search for "Prettier - Code formatter" and install it.

Then, within VS Code, go to **File / Preferences / Settings**. Select the **Workspace** tab, not the User tab. Search for "default formatter" and select the extension that we just installed, "Prettier - Code formatter".

The last step is to enable "formatOnSave" in VS Code. To do so, go to **File / Preferences / Settings**, select the Workspace tab, not the User tab. Search for "formatonsave". Then, click on the checkbox to select it.

By selecting the Workspace tab, we are specifying that we want the change to only be applied to the existing project that we're in and not any other projects.

If we take a closer look at the File Explorer in the left sidebar of VS Code, we will see a new folder named `.vscode` at the root level directory of the current project. This folder contains a file called `settings.json`. The settings that we applied at the Workspace level in VS Code can now be committed to a GitHub repository and shared with other developers. When other developers open the project in VS Code, they'll be able to work with the same VS Code settings as us. This makes collaborating on a project much simpler.

6. Set up ESlint

ESLint analyzes project code to quickly find problems with it. An `.eslintrc.cjs` file is already created for us by Vite.

If we check the `package.json` file, we can see that the following eslint-related packages have already been installed by Vite.

```
"@typescript-eslint/eslint-plugin": "^5.59.0",
"@typescript-eslint/parser": "^5.59.0",
"eslint": "^8.38.0",
"eslint-plugin-react-hooks": "^4.6.0",
"eslint-plugin-react-refresh": "^0.3.4",
```

Add React-specific linting rules for ESLint by running the following command: `yarn add -D eslint-plugin-react`.

Next, add an `.eslintignore` file. In this file, we can specify all the files that ESLint should ignore. Add the following lines to the new file.

```
node_modules/
dist/
.prettierrc.cjs
.eslintrc.cjs
```

Lastly, open the `.eslintrc.cjs` file. In the `extends` section, add configuration for the following:

```
"plugin:react/recommended",
"plugin:react/jsx-runtime",
// This disables the formatting rules in ESLint that Prettier is going to be
responsible for handling.
// Make sure it's always the last config, so it gets the chance to override o
ther configs.
"eslint-config-prettier";
```

In the `settings` section, add:

```
settings: {
  react: {
    // Tells eslint-plugin-react to automatically detect the version of React
to use.
    version: "detect"
  },
},
```

In the `rules` section, we can delete the `only-export-components` rule that Vite automatically added. We will be exporting more than just React components with React Router, so we probably don't want to be warned about this. Here is the line to delete:

```
'react-refresh/only-export-components': 'warn',
```

Basic routes

In this section, we will create a **Browser Router** and add some basic routes. This will enable client-side routing for the web app that we'll be building.

The Browser Router is the recommended router for all React Router web projects. It uses the *DOM History API* to update the URL and manage the history stack.

Our first route

Let's start by renaming the App.tsx file to Home.tsx.

```
export default function Home() {
  return <>Home</>;
}
```

Let's move the Home component to a new pages folder so that it has the following path: /src/pages/Home.tsx.

Then, let's create a Router.tsx file in the /src folder of our project. In this file, we will create a Browser Router and add our first route to the Home page.

```
import { createBrowserRouter } from "react-router-dom";
import Home from "./pages/Home";

const router = createBrowserRouter([
  {
    path: "/",
    element: <Home />,
  },
]);

export { router };
```

Since we want the Home page to be our root route, or main route, the path to it is just a forward slash.

Next, let's open the main.tsx project file, which is the main entry point to our app. Let's connect React Router to our app in this file. The main.tsx file will contain the following:

```
import React from 'react'
import ReactDOM from 'react-dom/client'
import App from './App.tsx'
import './index.css'

ReactDOM.createRoot(document.getElementById('root') as HTMLElement).render(
  <React.StrictMode>
    <App />
  </React.StrictMode>,
)
```

Let's replace the App component (which no longer exists) with a RouterProvider and then import the router that we defined in the Router.tsx file.

```
import React from 'react'
import ReactDOM from 'react-dom/client'
import { RouterProvider } from 'react-router-dom';
import { router } from './Router';
import './index.css'

ReactDOM.createRoot(document.getElementById('root') as HTMLElement).render(
  <React.StrictMode>
    <RouterProvider router={router} />
  </React.StrictMode>,
)
```

Now, let's run the yarn dev command. After doing so, we'll see a message in the terminal that will tell us to go to http://127.0.0.1:5173/ in order to view our app. We can also use http://localhost:5173/. The root route will be rendered, which is the Home page that we defined.

Adding a second route

Let's add a new page, an About page. First, let's create a component for it in the pages folder.

```
export default function About() {
  return <>About</>;
}
```

Then, let's update the Router.tsx file to include a route for the About component.

```
import { createBrowserRouter } from "react-router-dom";
import Home from "./pages/Home";
import About from "./pages/About";

const router = createBrowserRouter([
```

```
  {
    path: "/",
    element: <Home />,
  },
  {
    path: "about",
    element: <About />,
  },
]);

export { router };
```

Now, if we try navigating to `http://127.0.0.1:5173/about`, we will see the new About page that we created.

However, if we try navigating to `http://127.0.0.1:5173/contact` or any other non-existent page, we will get the following error:

```
Unexpected Application Error!
404 Not Found
◉ Hey developer ✋

You can provide a way better UX than this when your app throws errors by prov
iding your own ErrorBoundary or errorElement prop on your route.
```

This is React Router's default *404 Not Found* page. Let's see how we can create our own custom *404 Not Found* error page.

Adding a custom 404 page

Let's add a custom 404 page by creating a new *catch-all* route within our router. The `path` for a catch-all route must have the asterisk symbol. It caches and handles any route that doesn't match all the defined routes. Then, let's define an inline React component as the route's element for the custom 404 page.

```
import { createBrowserRouter, Link } from "react-router-dom";
import Home from "./pages/Home";
import About from "./pages/About";

const router = createBrowserRouter([
  {
    path: "/",
    element: <Home />,
```

```
    },
    {
      path: "about",
      element: <About />,
    },
    {
      path: "*",
      element: (
        <>
          <h1>Not found</h1>
          <Link to="/">Back home</Link>
        </>
      ),
    },
]);

export { router };
```

We used the React Router `<Link>` component to create a link back to the home page. The `<Link>` component allows us to achieve client-side routing. The app updates the URL without requesting another document from the server. The app immediately renders the user interface for the route that the user navigates to via `<Link>`.

Notice that we didn't create and import a React component for the catch-all route. If the component won't ever be used again in the app, this approach can work. However, it's always best to create an isolated component for each route. This will make the component easier to read, document, test, and debug.

Let's create a standalone React component for our 404 page. Within the pages folder, create a NotFound.tsx file with the following component in it:

```
import { Link } from "react-router-dom";

export default function NotFound() {
  return (
    <>
      <header>
        <h1>Not found</h1>
      </header>
      <section>
        <Link to="/">Back home</Link>
      </section>
    </>
  );
}
```

Next, let's update the catch-all route of our router to reference the NotFound component that we just created.

```
import { createBrowserRouter } from "react-router-dom";
import Home from "./pages/Home";
import About from "./pages/About";
import NotFound from "./pages/NotFound";

const router = createBrowserRouter([
  {
    path: "/",
    element: <Home />,
  },
  {
    path: "about",
    element: <About />,
  },
  {
    path: "*",
    element: <NotFound />,
  },
]);

export { router };
```

Let's try visiting a route that does not exist, such as http://localhost:5173/contact, to see our custom 404 page in action. The NotFound component that we created is now displayed as our custom 404 page. Click on the *Back home* link to go back to the main page.

Nested routes

Nested routes are a powerful feature made available to us by React Router. Nested routing allows us to load specific parts of a user interface based on the route that the user navigates to.

Nested routes are great for building layout templates for various parts of our app. Our app's public routes can be nested within a *main layout* template while our protected administrative routes can be nested within a *dashboard layout* template. Nested routing allows us to configure consistent layouts across groups of pages in our app.

For another example of nested routing, consider a page with multiple tabs (ex: Laptops, Desktops). Clicking on a tab will update the URL in the browser accordingly. Nested routing can allow us to replace the content of the current tab without replacing the entire page.

Layout route

Nested routing is often used to create a consistent layout across all of a site's pages. We can achieve this with a layout route.

Before diving into layout routes, let's look at a very basic way to create a consistent layout using React's `children` prop. Let's create a Layout component in a `/src/components/Layout.tsx` file.

```
type Props = {
  children: React.ReactNode,
};

export default function Layout({ children }: Props) {
  return <main>{children}</main>;
}
```

With the Layout component now created, we can now apply it to our pages.

```
import { createBrowserRouter } from "react-router-dom";
import Home from "./pages/Home";
import About from "./pages/About";
import NotFound from "./pages/NotFound";
import Layout from "./components/Layout";

const router = createBrowserRouter([
```

```
  {
    path: "/",
    element: (
      <Layout>
        <Home />
      </Layout>
    ),
  },
  {
    path: "about",
    element: (
      <Layout>
        <About />
      </Layout>
    ),
  },
  {
    path: "*",
    element: (
      <Layout>
        <NotFound />
      </Layout>
    ),
  },
]);

export { router };
```

One issue with the above code is that there is a lot of repetition going on with the Layout component. The Layout component has to be repeated for every route.

A better solution is to use a layout route. A layout route is not an actual route that we'll navigate to. It's simply a way to give a group of routes the same layout.

Let's update the Layout component to use React Router's Outlet component instead of the children prop.

```
import { Outlet } from "react-router-dom";

export default function Layout() {
  return (
    <main>
      <Outlet />
    </main>
  );
}
```

The Outlet component injects the component that belongs to the matching route. If the matching route is the /about route, the About component will be injected into the Outlet.

Let's nest the pages of our app within the layout route. These pages will be child routes of the parent layout route. Here's what these changes look like in Router.tsx.

```tsx
import { createBrowserRouter } from "react-router-dom";
import Home from "./pages/Home";
import About from "./pages/About";
import NotFound from "./pages/NotFound";
import Layout from "./components/Layout";

const router = createBrowserRouter([
  {
    path: "/",
    element: <Layout />,
    children: [
      {
        index: true,
        element: <Home />,
      },
      {
        path: "about",
        element: <About />,
      },
      {
        path: "*",
        element: <NotFound />,
      },
    ],
  },
]);

export { router };
```

We set the index property to true for the route that loads the Home component. This makes it an index route. An index route is the default child route. An index route will render into its parent's Outlet at its parent's URL. Therefore, when we try navigating to the / route, the index route will render, displaying the Home component within the Layout.

Adding a site header and footer

Let's create a more realistic Layout component by adding a global site header and site footer to it. This will allow the site header and site footer to appear on every page.

Create a new `/src/components/Header.tsx` file and add the following component to it:

```tsx
import { Link } from "react-router-dom";
import { siteConfig } from "../config/site";

export default function Header() {
  return (
    <header className="sticky w-full border-b shadow-sm backdrop-blur">
      <div className="container flex items-center h-14 mx-auto">
        <div className="flex items-center space-x-6 md:gap-10">
          <Link to="/">
            <h1 className="font-bold">{siteConfig.name}</h1>
          </Link>
          <nav>
            <Link to="/about">About</Link>
          </nav>
        </div>
      </div>
    </header>
  );
}
```

We created a `/src/config/index.ts` file to store configuration settings for our app, such as the store name. This helps us to avoid hard coding the store name in multiple places across the site. It will be easier to modify our store name in the future.

```ts
export const siteConfig = {
  name: "My Store",
};
```

Create a new `/src/components/Footer.tsx` file and add the following component to it:

```tsx
import { Link } from "react-router-dom";
import { siteConfig } from "../config/site";

export default function Footer() {
  return (
    <footer className="border-t py-6 md:py-0">
      <div className="container mx-auto flex flex-col items-center md:h-16 md:flex-row">
        <p className="text-center text-sm md:text-left">
          &copy;{" "}
          <Link to="/" className="underline-offset-4 hover:underline">
            {siteConfig.name}
          </Link>
          .
        </p>
      </div>
```

```
      </footer>
  );
}
```

Now, let's update the Layout component to include the Header and Footer components.

```
import { Outlet } from "react-router-dom";
import Footer from "./Footer";
import Header from "./Header";

export default function Layout() {
  return (
    <main className="flex flex-col min-h-screen">
      <Header />
      <div className="container mx-auto py--24">
        <Outlet />
      </div>
      <Footer />
    </main>
  );
}
```

We added a few TailwindCSS classes to style our main element. The flex and flex-col

classes applies a flexbox layout with a column direction. The min-h-screen class sets the min-height

of the element to 100% of the viewport height.

We also added a few TailwindCSS classes to the div that wraps the Outlet. The container

class automatically sets the max-width of the main element depending on the current screen size, or

the current breakpoint. The mx-auto class centers our container, and the py-24 class adds vertical

padding.

Nested dashboard routes

Let's create a dashboard area for the store app that we're building. The dashboard will be an

administrative area where we can create, view, edit, and delete products.

Let's start by creating a DashboardLayout component that will serve as the layout for the

entire dashboard and its sub-pages. Create this component in a new

/src/components/DashboardLayout.tsx file.

```
import { Outlet, Link } from "react-router-dom";
import Footer from "./Footer";
```

```
import Header from "./Header";

export default function DashboardLayout() {
  return (
    <main className="relative flex min-h-screen flex-col">
      <Header />
      <section className="container mx-auto">
        <div className="my-12 grid gap-12 md:grid-cols-[200px_1fr]">
          <nav className="space-y-3 md:w-[200px]">
            <h2 className="text-lg font-semibold">Dashboard Menu</h2>
            <ul className="space-y-3">
              <li>
                <Link to="/dashboard/products" className="underline">
                  Products
                </Link>
              </li>
              <li>
                <Link to="/dashboard" className="underline">
                  Back to Dashboard
                </Link>
              </li>
            </ul>
          </nav>
          <div>
            <Outlet />
          </div>
        </div>
      </section>
      <Footer />
    </main>
  );
}
```

In this component, we used CSS Grid via TailwindCSS classes to create a two-column layout. The first column contains a dashboard menu, and the second column contains the page that we render within the Outlet. At smaller screen sizes, the two-column layout collapses to become a one-column layout.

The dashboard menu contains two menu options. The first menu option links to a new /dashboard/products route that we will create. The second menu option provides a link to go back to a main /dashboard page, no matter where the user is in the dashboard.

Dashboard pages

Let's create the main dashboard page component in a new
`/src/pages/dashboard/DashboardIndex.tsx` file. To keep things simple, this component will just welcome the user to the dashboard.

```tsx
export default function DashboardIndex() {
  return (
    <div className="space-y-12">
      <header>
        <h1 className="font-bold text-3xl md:text-4xl">Dashboard</h1>
        <p className="text-lg">Store dashboard.</p>
      </header>
      <p>Welcome to your dashboard.</p>
    </div>
  );
}
```

Let's create the dashboard's products page component in a new
`/src/pages/dashboard/DashboardProducts.tsx` file. We don't have any products to display right now, but we will soon.

```tsx
export default function DashboardProducts() {
  return (
    <div className="space-y-12">
      <header>
        <h1 className="font-bold text-3xl md:text-4xl">Products</h1>
        <p className="text-lg">Listing of products.</p>
      </header>
      <section>Coming soon.</section>
    </div>
  );
}
```

Dashboard routes

Next, let's create a new route in the `Router.tsx` file with the `path` set to `dashboard` and the `element` set to the `DashboardLayout` component. Then, let's add a `children` property that will contain the following:

- A main dashboard page, represented by the `DashboardIndex` page component.

- A dashboard products page to view and manage products, represented by the DashboardProducts page component.

```
import { createBrowserRouter } from "react-router-dom";
import Home from "./pages/Home";
import NotFound from "./pages/NotFound";
import DashboardIndex from "./pages/dashboard/DashboardIndex";
import DashboardProducts from "./pages/dashboard/DashboardProducts";
import Layout from "./components/Layout";
import DashboardLayout from "./components/DashboardLayout";

const router = createBrowserRouter([
  {
    path: "/",
    element: <Layout />,
    children: [
      {
        index: true,
        element: <Home />,
      },
      {
        path: "about",
        element: <About />,
      },
      {
        path: "*",
        element: <NotFound />,
      },
    ],
  },
  {
    path: "dashboard",
    element: <DashboardLayout />,
    children: [
      {
        index: true,
        element: <DashboardIndex />,
      },
      {
        path: "products",
        element: <DashboardProducts />,
      },
    ],
  },
]);

export { router };
```

We set the `index` property to `true` for the `DashboardIndex` component. This makes it the main page of the dashboard section of our app. When we go to the `/dashboard` route, without using any sub-path in the URL, the `DashboardIndex` component will be displayed.

When we navigate to the `/dashboard` route, we see the `DashboardIndex` page component rendered. When we navigate to the `/dashboard/products` route, we see the `DashboardProducts` page component rendered.

When we navigate to a non-existent route, such as `/dashboard/account`, we see the `NotFound` component. React Router's nested routing capabilities makes it very easy for us to create different sections of our app and apply different layouts to them.

Header dashboard link

Let's add a link to the dashboard in the main menu of the `Header` component. Ideally, this link should only be displayed when a user with the right permissions is signed-in. For now, we'll just start by making it always visible.

```
import { Link } from "react-router-dom";
import { siteConfig } from "../config/site";

export default function Header() {
  return (
    <header className="sticky w-full border-b shadow-sm backdrop-blur">
      <div className="container flex items-center justify-between h-14 mx-aut
o">
        <div className="flex items-center space-x-6 md:gap-10">
          <Link to="/">
            <h1 className="font-bold">{siteConfig.name}</h1>
          </Link>
          <nav>
            <Link to="/about">About</Link>
          </nav>
        </div>
        <div>
          <Link to="/dashboard">Dashboard</Link>
        </div>
      </div>
    </header>
  );
}
```

Managing products

In this section, we'll use React Router to enrich our dashboard area. We'll make it possible for store administrators to create, view, edit, and delete products. We'll learn how to:

- Use React Router `loader` functions

- Use React Router `action` functions

- Submit forms with React Router

- Validate forms

- Handle errors

Product types

To start managing products in our online store app, let's start by creating the TypeScript types that we'll need. Create a `/src/types/index.d.ts` file. A `.d.ts` file is a type declaration file that contains only TypeScript type information.

We'll define a `Product` type with information that we want to track for each product. Then, we'll define a `ProductDto` type that we'll use for the data transfer object of the product creation form. The `ProductDto` type will be based on the `Product` type, but will omit fields that don't apply to the data submitted by the product creation form.

We'll also define a `EditProductDto` that we'll use for the data transfer object of the edit product form. The `EditProductDto` will be based on `ProductDto`, but it will be a `Partial` of it. The TypeScript `Partial` marks all fields as optional.

The `EditProductDto` will allow us to be more flexible when updating products. Since all fields are optional, we can simply update the field(s) we need to. This will come in handy later when we add a product wishlist feature, allowing users to add or remove products from their wishlist. With all `EditProductDto` fields as optional, we'll be able to update only the `isInWishlist` boolean field.

```
export type Product = {
  id: string,
  title: string,
  description?: string,
```

```
  price: number,
  brand: string,
  category: string,
  imageUrl: string,
  isInWishlist?: boolean,
  createdAt: number,
};

export type ProductDto = Omit<Product, "id" | "createdAt">;

export type EditProductDto = Partial<ProductDto>;
```

The API

We'll need an API to send our requests to create, read, update, and delete products. Rather than building out an entire API service and making network requests to it, which is beyond the scope of this book, we can create a fake API using localStorage.

Using localStorage will allow us to save data as key/value pairs in the browser. The data will have no expiration time, unless we choose to clear our browsing data in the browser.

We'll add a fakeNetworkRequest function to add some artificial network delay for every function in our fake API. This will make the API seem more realistic. Then, we'll add functions to fetch all products, fetch one product, add a product, edit a product, and delete a product.

Add the following code in a new /src/utils/fake-api.ts file.

```typescript
import { EditProductDto, Product, ProductDto } from "../types";

// fake a network request
async function fakeNetworkRequest() {
  return new Promise((resolve) => {
    setTimeout(resolve, Math.random() * 700);
  });
}

export async function getProducts(searchTerm?: string): Promise<Product[]> {
  await fakeNetworkRequest();

  const products = localStorage.getItem("products");

  if (!products) {
    return [];
  }
```

```typescript
  let productsList: Product[] = JSON.parse(products);

  if (searchTerm) {
    productsList = productsList.filter((product) =>
      product.title.includes(searchTerm)
    );
  }

  return productsList.sort((a: Product, b: Product) => {
    if (a.title < b.title) {
      return -1;
    }
    if (a.title > b.title) {
      return 1;
    }
    return 0;
  });
}

export async function addProduct(data: ProductDto): Promise<Product> {
  await fakeNetworkRequest();

  const id = Math.random().toString(36).substring(2, 9);
  const product = { id, createdAt: Date.now(), ...data };

  const products = await getProducts();
  products.unshift(product);
  localStorage.setItem("products", JSON.stringify(products));

  return product;
}

export async function getProduct(id: string): Promise<Product | null> {
  await fakeNetworkRequest();

  const products = localStorage.getItem("products");

  if (!products) {
    return null;
  }

  const product = JSON.parse(products).find(
    (product: Product) => product.id === id
  );

  return product ?? null;
}

export async function editProduct(
```

```typescript
  id: string,
  data: EditProductDto
): Promise<Product> {
  await fakeNetworkRequest();
  const products = localStorage.getItem("products");

  if (!products) {
    throw new Error("No products found.");
  }

  const productsList: Product[] = JSON.parse(products);
  const product: Product | undefined = productsList.find(
    (product: Product) => product.id === id
  );

  if (!product) {
    throw new Error("Product not found.");
  }

  const updatedProduct: Product = { ...product, ...data };
  const existingProducts: Product[] = productsList.filter(
    (product: Product) => product.id !== id
  );

  localStorage.setItem(
    "products",
    JSON.stringify([...existingProducts, updatedProduct])
  );

  return updatedProduct;
}

export async function deleteProduct(id: string): Promise<Product> {
  const products = localStorage.getItem("products");

  if (!products) {
    throw new Error("No products found.");
  }

  const productsList: Product[] = JSON.parse(products);
  const index = productsList.findIndex(
    (product: Product) => product.id.toLowerCase() === id.toLowerCase()
  );

  if (index === -1) {
    throw new Error("Product not found.");
  }

  const deletedProduct = productsList.splice(index, 1);
  localStorage.setItem("products", JSON.stringify(productsList));
```

```
    return deletedProduct[0];
}
```

Get products

To retrieve and display the list of products, we'll need to update the DashboardProducts component. Let's define a React Router loader function just above the component declaration. This loader function will call the getProducts function from our API.

Each route in our app can define a loader function to provide data to the component for the route before it renders. A loader function is an asynchronous function that returns a Promise.

```
export async function loader(): Promise<{ products: Product[] }> {
  const products = await getProducts();
  return { products };
}
```

Next, let's use React Router's useLoaderData Hook inside our component DashboardProducts component. This Hook makes the value that we returned from the loader function above available to our component.

```
import { useLoaderData } from 'react-router-dom';
import { siteConfig } from '../../config/site';
import ProductsList from '../../components/ProductsList';

export async function loader(): Promise<{ products: Product[] }> {
  const products = await getProducts();
  return { products };
}

export default function DashboardProducts() {
  const { products } = useLoaderData() as Awaited<ReturnType<typeof loader>>;

  return (
    <div className="space-y-12">
      <header>
        <h1 className="font-bold text-3xl md:text-4xl">Products</h1>
        <p className="text-lg">Listing of products.</p>
      </header>
      <ProductsList products={products} />
    </div>
  );
}
```

You'll notice that we used a `ProductsList` component within `DashboardProducts`. Let's create a new `/src/components/ProductsList.tsx` file and add the following code to it.

```tsx
import { Product } from "../types";
import ProductCard from "./ProductCard";

type Props = {
  products: Product[],
};

export default function ProductsList({ products }: Props) {
  return (
    <>
      {products.length ? (
        <div className="grid grid-cols-1 lg:grid-cols-3 gap-6">
          {products.map((product) => (
            <ProductCard key={product.id} product={product} />
          ))}
        </div>
      ) : (
        <p className="bg-gray-50 border text-gray-500 p-6 rounded-lg">
          No products found.
        </p>
      )}
    </>
  );
}
```

The `ProductsList` component receives an array of products. If the array contains products, it displays the products using CSS Grid via TailwindCSS classes. Each individual product is represented by a `ProductCard` component that we will create next. If the array contains no products, then we return a message to let the user know.

Let's create a new `/src/components/ProductCard.tsx` file and add the following code to it.

```tsx
import { Link } from "react-router-dom";
import { Product } from "../types";

type Props = {
  product: Product,
};

export default function ProductCard({ product }: Props) {
  return (
    <article className="border rounded-lg p-3 space-y-4 shadow-lg">
```

```
      <div className="relative aspect-square">
        <Link to={`/dashboard/products/${product.id}`}>
          <img
            src={product.imageUrl}
            className="object-cover aspect-square rounded-t-lg"
          />
        </Link>
      </div>
      <div className="space-y-2">
        <h3 className="text-lg font-medium">
          <Link to={`/dashboard/products/${product.id}`}>{product.title}</Lin
k>
        </h3>
        <p className="text-sm">{product.description}</p>
      </div>
    </article>
  );
}
```

The ProductCard component displays an individual product in a card layout that we defined using TailwindCSS classes. This component contains links to a single product page that we'll soon create within the dashboard. This page will be where we'll be able to manage each product.

Error page

What happens if an error occurs in the loader function within DashboardProducts? Let's find out. Let's throw an error from the loader function.

```
export async function loader(): Promise<{ products: Product[] }> {
  throw new Error("My error");
  const products = await getProducts();
  return { products };
}
```

Now, let's reload the dashboard products page. We'll see the following.

```
Unexpected Application Error!
My error
...
◎ Hey developer 👋
You can provide a way better UX than this when your app throws errors by prov
iding your own ErrorBoundary or errorElement prop on your route.
```

Any time that our app throws an error while rendering, while loading data in a `loader` function, or while performing data mutations, React Router will catch it and render the default error screen that we saw above. This error screen is cryptic for users.

We can make error handling more user-friendly by creating a custom error page. We can then set it as the error page for a route by using the `errorElement` route property.

Let's create the error page component in a new `/src/pages/Error.tsx` file. Add the following code to this new file.

```tsx
import { isRouteErrorResponse, useRouteError } from "react-router-dom";

export default function ErrorPage() {
  const error = useRouteError();
  let errorMessage;

  if (isRouteErrorResponse(error)) {
    errorMessage = (
      <p>
        {error.status} {error.statusText}
      </p>
    );
  } else if (error instanceof Error) {
    errorMessage = error.message || "Unknown Error";
  }

  return (
    <div className="space-y-6">
      <header>
        <h1 className="font-bold text-3xl md:text-4xl">Oops!</h1>
        <p className="text-lg">An error occurred.</p>
      </header>
      <section className="space-y-6">
        <p>Sorry, an unexpected error has occurred.</p>
        <p>
          <i>{errorMessage}</i>
        </p>
      </section>
    </div>
  );
}
```

The `ErrorPage` component uses our own custom styling to display the error that occurred. We used React Router's `useRouteError` Hook to retrieve the error that is thrown. An error can occur within a `loader` function, an `action` function, or it can occur while rendering the component.

The `error` type returned by `useRouteError` is unknown. Therefore, we used React Router's `isRouteErrorResponse` method to check if the given error is of type `ErrorResponse`. The `ErrorResponse` type is generated by React Router for a *4xx/5xx Response* thrown from an `action` or `loader` function. If the error is of type `ErrorResponse`, then we can retrieve the `status` and `statusText` properties from the `error`. If not, it must be a general `Error`, in which case we can retrieve the `message` property from it.

Next, we need to set our new `ErrorPage` as the `errorElement` on the `DashboardProducts` route in the `Router.tsx` file.

```
//...

import ErrorPage from './pages/Error';

//...

{
  path: 'products',
  element: <DashboardProducts />,
  loader: dashboardProductsLoader,
  errorElement: <ErrorPage />,
}
```

Now, when we refresh the dashboard products page, we see our custom error page. The user can continue to interact with the parts of the page that aren't having trouble, such as the dashboard sidebar menu and the main site header. We've created an error boundary that exists only around the `DashboardProducts` portion of the page.

Errors bubble up to the nearest `errorElement`. If we had set the `errorElement` on the dashboard route rather than the `dashboard/products` route, then the error would have bubbled up to that `errorElement`. However, one drawback of doing so is that the error page would have taken up the entire content area, including the dashboard sidebar menu.

Single product page

Let's create a page component to view a single product. We will be taken to this new page when we click on a product from the dashboard's products page. Create a `DashboardProduct` page component in a new `/src/pages/dashboard/DashboardProduct.tsx` file.

The goal of this page is to display the details of a single product. Later on, we will add "Edit" and "Delete" buttons to this page in order to manage the product listing.

```tsx
import { ParamParseKey, Params, useLoaderData, Navigate } from 'react-router-dom';
import { siteConfig } from '../../config/site';
import { Product } from '../../types';

const path = 'dashboard/products/:productId';

export async function loader({
  params: { productId },
}: {
  params: Params<ParamParseKey<typeof path>>;
}): Promise<Product | null> {
  if (productId) {
    return getProduct(productId);
  }

  return null;
}

export default function DashboardProduct() {
  const product = useLoaderData() as Awaited<ReturnType<typeof loader>>;

  if (!product) {
    return <Navigate to="/dashboard/products" replace={true} />;
  }

  return (
    <div className="space-y-12">
      <header className="space-y-2">
        <h1 className="font-bold text-3xl md:text-4xl">{product.title}</h1>
        <p className="text-lg">{product.description}</p>
      </header>
      <aside>
        <img src={product.imageUrl} />
      </aside>
      <section>
        <dl className="space-y-4">
          <div>
            <dt className="font-medium">Brand</dt>
            <dd>{product.brand}</dd>
          </div>
          <div>
            <dt className="font-medium">Category</dt>
            <dd>{product.category}</dd>
          </div>
          <div>
```

```
        <dt className="font-medium">Price</dt>
        <dd>{product.price}</dd>
      </div>
    </dl>
  </section>
</div>
  );
}
```

When routing to a single product page, we need to use *dynamic routing*. Dynamic routing is routing that takes place as our app is rendering.

The route for the single product page will be `products/:productId`. The colon (:) turns the URL segment into a *dynamic segment*. Dynamic segments will match dynamic (changing) values in that position of the URL. The `productId` URL segment will receive the ID for a specific product. Values such as `productId` in the URL are often called *URL params* or just *params*.

The `productId` URL param is passed to the route's `loader` function. The `loader` function reads from the dynamic `productId` segment in the URL. If no `productId` is found, the `loader` function returns `null`. We pass the `productId` to the `getProduct` function from our API in order to return the details of the product whose `id` matches the `productId`.

We use the `useLoaderData` Hook inside the component to make the product data available for display. If no product is found for the given `productId`, we render the React Router `Navigate` component that redirects the user to the provided route, which we set to be the dashboard products page.

Single product route

Let's add a new route for the new single product page within the `Router.tsx` file. This route will have its `path` set to `products/:productId` within the child routes of the dashboard. We'll set the `loader` of the route to point to the `loader` function that we created above the `DashboardProduct` component. We'll also set the `errorElement` for this route.

```
import { createBrowserRouter } from "react-router-dom";
import DashboardProducts, {
  loader as dashboardProductsLoader,
} from "./pages/dashboard/DashboardProducts";
import DashboardLayout from "./components/DashboardLayout";
import ErrorPage from "./pages/Error";
```

```
import DashboardProduct, {
  loader as dashboardProductLoader,
} from "./pages/dashboard/DashboardProduct";
//...

const router = createBrowserRouter([
  {
    //...
  },
  {
    path: "/dashboard",
    element: <DashboardLayout />,
    children: [
      //...
      {
        path: "products",
        element: <DashboardProducts />,
        loader: dashboardProductsLoader,
        errorElement: <ErrorPage />,
      },
      {
        path: "products/:productId",
        element: <DashboardProduct />,
        loader: dashboardProductLoader,
        errorElement: <ErrorPage />,
      },
      //...
    ],
  },
]);

export { router };
```

Now, when we click on a product from the dashboard products page, we are taken to the new single product page that we just created.

ErrorPage as a pathless route

As you may have noticed, we are now repeating errorElement on multiple dashboard routes with the same ErrorPage. This solution works fine but it's not very elegant. Since the same ErrorPage is used for multiple routes, there's a better solution. We can reuse the same error page across all dashboard routes by using what is called a *pathless route*.

Routes can be used without a path. These pathless routes will be part of the app's UI layout without requiring new path segments in the URL.

Let's update our router to use a pathless route for the `ErrorPage`. Within the `children` property of the dashboard route, add a new pathless route with the `errorElement` property set to `<ErrorPage />`. Give this pathless route its own `children` property. Then, move the dashboard routes to the `children` property of the pathless route. Below is what these changes will look like.

```
import { createBrowserRouter } from "react-router-dom";
import Layout from "./components/Layout";
import ErrorPage from "./pages/Error";
import DashboardLayout from "./components/DashboardLayout";
import DashboardIndex from "./pages/dashboard/DashboardIndex";
import DashboardProducts, {
  loader as dashboardProductsLoader,
} from "./pages/dashboard/DashboardProducts";
import DashboardProduct, {
  loader as dashboardProductLoader,
} from "./pages/dashboard/DashboardProduct";
//...

const router = createBrowserRouter([
  {
    path: "/",
    element: <Layout />,
    children: [
      //...
    ],
  },
  {
    path: "/dashboard",
    element: <DashboardLayout />,
    children: [
      {
        errorElement: <ErrorPage />,
        children: [
          {
            index: true,
            element: <DashboardIndex />,
          },
          {
            path: "products",
            element: <DashboardProducts />,
            loader: dashboardProductsLoader,
          },
          {
            path: "products/:productId",
            element: <DashboardProduct />,
            loader: dashboardProductLoader,
          },
        ],
```

```
      },
    ],
  },
]);

export { router };
```

When an error is thrown from any of the dashboard routes, the ErrorPage will be rendered without us having to configure the errorElement property on every dashboard route.

Creating products

Let's add the functionality to create new products. First, let's insert an "Add New" link on the dashboard products page. This link will direct us to a new /dashboard/products/new route for a product creation page that we'll create shortly. This new product creation page will contain a form to add new products.

```
import { Link, useLoaderData } from "react-router-dom";
//...

export async function loader(): Promise<{ products: Product[] }> {
  //...
}

export default function DashboardProducts() {
  const { products } = useLoaderData() as Awaited<ReturnType<typeof loader>>;

  return (
    <div className="space-y-12">
      <header className="flex items-center justify-between">
        <div>
          <h1 className="font-bold text-3xl md:text-4xl">Products</h1>
          <p className="text-lg">Listing of products.</p>
        </div>
        <Link
          to="/dashboard/products/new"
          className="bg-black hover:bg-gray-800 px-4 py-2 rounded text-white"
        >
          Add New
        </Link>
      </header>
      <ProductsList products={products} />
    </div>
  );
}
```

Create product page

Let's create a new `DashboardNewProduct` page component in a new
`/src/pages/dashboard/DashboardNewProduct.tsx` file. Add the following code to it.

```
import { Form, redirect } from "react-router-dom";
import { siteConfig } from "../../config/site";

export default function DashboardNewProduct() {
  return (
    <div className="space-y-12">
      <header>
        <h1 className="font-bold text-3xl md:text-4xl">New Product</h1>
        <p className="text-lg">Create a new product.</p>
      </header>
      <Form method="post" className="space-y-6">
        <label className="flex flex-col space-y-1">
          <span className="font-medium">Product title</span>
          <input
            type="text"
            name="title"
            required
            className="border p-2 rounded"
          />
        </label>
        <label className="flex flex-col space-y-1">
          <span className="font-medium">Product description</span>
          <textarea name="description" className="border p-2 rounded" />
        </label>
        <label className="flex flex-col space-y-1">
          <span className="font-medium">Price</span>
          <input
            type="text"
            name="price"
            required
            className="border p-2 rounded"
          />
        </label>
        <label className="flex flex-col space-y-1">
          <span className="font-medium">Brand</span>
          <input
            type="text"
            name="brand"
            required
            className="border p-2 rounded"
          />
        </label>
        <label className="flex flex-col space-y-1">
```

```
            <span className="font-medium">Category</span>
            <input
              type="text"
              name="category"
              required
              className="border p-2 rounded"
            />
          </label>
          <label className="flex flex-col space-y-1">
            <span className="font-medium">Image URL</span>
            <input
              type="text"
              name="imageUrl"
              required
              className="border p-2 rounded"
            />
          </label>
          <div>
            <button
              type="submit"
              className="bg-black hover:bg-gray-800 px-4 py-2 rounded text-whit
e"
            >
              Save
            </button>
          </div>
        </Form>
      </div>
    );
}
```

Instead of using the default HTML <form> element for the product creation form, we are using

the React Router <Form> element. The <Form> element provides us with a simple way of performing

data mutations in an app powered by React Router. These data mutations include creating, updating,

and deleting data.

HTML forms actually cause a navigation to happen in the browser, just like clicking a link. While

links change the URL, forms can also change the request method (GET, POST, PUT, PATCH, DELETE) and

the request body (form data).

The React Router <Form> element prevents the default browser behavior of sending a new

POST request to the server. Instead, it sends the form submission to the route action function, which

we'll learn about next.

We set the method of the <Form> to POST because the HTTP POST method is used to create a new resource, which is what we want here, to create new products. The method property of the <Form> determines the HTTP verb to be used when submitting the form. While the plain HTML <form> only supports GET and POST, React Router's <Form> also supports PUT, PATCH, and DELETE. If no method is provided, the default is GET.

<Form> submissions with a method of POST have their form data put into the request POST body. <Form> submissions with a method of GET will not call an action function. GET submissions are like normal navigation (ex: user clicks a link). When submitted, the browser creates the request for the next document, putting the form data as URLSearchParams in the URL.

If we use the HTML <form> with a method of post, the browser will automatically serialize the form's data and send it to the server as the request body for the POST request. However, our Vite server isn't configured to handle a POST request so we'll get a HTTP Error 404. Instead of sending the request to the server, the React Router <Form> uses client-side routing to send the request to the route's action function.

The React Router <Form> element provides us with some other advantages too:

- Even if JavaScript is disabled in the user's browser, data interactions created with <Form> and action functions (our next topic) will work.

- After a <Form> submission, if there is a loader function for that page, the loader function will be reloaded. This allows any data updates to be immediately reflected in the UI.

- <Form> automatically serializes the form values (which is what the browser does even when JavaScript is disabled). This automatic serialization allows us to use the formData method of the Request interface to read the request body containing the data submitted by our form.

The product creation action

A route loader is for reading data, and a route action is for writing data. Route action functions allow us to perform data mutations (ex: POST, PUT, PATCH, DELETE) using simple HTML and HTTP.

Let's add an `action` function above the `DashboardNewProduct` component. It will handle the posting of data by the `<Form>` that we defined in the component.

```
export async function action({ request }: { request: Request }) {
  const errors: { [key: string]: string } = {};

  try {
    const formData = await request.formData();

    const title = formData.get('title') as string;
    const description = formData.get('description') as string;
    const price = formData.get('price') as string;
    const brand = formData.get('brand') as string;
    const category = formData.get('category') as string;
    const imageUrl = formData.get('imageUrl') as string;

    await addProduct({
      title,
      description,
      price: parseFloat(price),
      brand,
      category,
      imageUrl,
    });

    return redirect(`/dashboard/products`);
  } catch (e) {
    errors.form = 'Product creation failed. Please try again later.';
    return { errors };
  }
}

export default function DashboardNewProduct() {
  return (
    //...
  )
}
```

When the `<Form method="post">` is submitted, the POST request body is returned as a promise that we can retrieve with `request.formData()`. This promise resolves as a `FormData` object. We retrieve each field's data from the `FormData` object and then pass this data to our API's `addProduct` function.

After the new product is created, we redirect the user back to the dashboard products page.

If an error occurs during new product creation, we return an `errors` object from the `action` function. We assigned the error message to the `form` key of the `errors` object, to denote that this is a form-wide error, not an error relating to a specific form field.

To test the error handling, we can add `throw new Error()` as the first line in the `try` block. We won't see anything yet because we are not displaying any errors in the component. Let's do that next.

Let's use the React Router `useActionData` Hook within our `DashboardNewProduct` component to retrieve the `errors` object and display a form-wide error message when `errors.form` has been set.

```
import { Form, redirect, useActionData } from 'react-router-dom';
import { addProduct } from '../../utils/fake-api';

export async function action({ request }: { request: Request }) {
  const errors: { [key: string]: string } = {};

  try {
    // simulate an error
    throw new Error()

    //...
  } catch (e) {
    errors.form = 'Product creation failed. Please try again later.';
    return { errors };
  }
```

```
}

export default function DashboardNewProduct() {
  const actionData = useActionData() as { errors: { [key: string]: string } }
;
  const { errors } = actionData ?? {};

  return (
    <div className="space-y-12">
      <header>
        <h1 className="font-bold text--3xl md:text-4xl">New Product</h1>
        <p className="text-lg">Create a new product.</p>
      </header>

      {errors?.form && <div className="bg-red-50 p-3 rounded text-red-800">{e
rrors?.form}</div>}

      <Form method="post" className="space-y-6">
        {/* ... */}
      </Form>
    </div>
  );
}
```

Now, when we simulate the throwing of an error from the `try` block in the `action` function, we see an error message displayed above the form.

Actions and multiple form methods

We've seen how an `action` function handles a single form `method` of `post`. What if we had multiple React Router `<Form>` elements on a single page with a different `method` set for each one? Could we handle all the different form submissions in one `action` function? Yes we can.

The `method` is available from the `request` object that the `action` function receives. We can retrieve the `method` to perform different logic based on which `<Form>` was submitted.

Let's try this out on a new test page. We'll add a new route for our test page and set its `element` to a `FormsTest` page component that we'll create next. We'll set the route's `action` to an action function that we'll also create next.

```
import FormsTest, { action as formsTestAction } from "./pages/FormsTest";

//...
```

```
<Route path="/forms-test" element={<FormsTest />} action={formsTestAction} />
;
```

Let's create the FormsTest component in a new /src/pages/FormsTest file.

```
import { Form } from "react-router-dom";

export async function action({ request }: { request: Request }) {
  switch (request.method) {
    case "GET": {
      console.log("GET");
      return null;
    }
    case "POST": {
      console.log("POST");
      return null;
    }
    case "PUT": {
      console.log("PUT");
      return null;
    }
    case "PATCH": {
      console.log("PATCH");
      return null;
    }
    case "DELETE": {
      console.log("DELETE");
      return null;
    }
    default: {
      throw new Error("Method not found.");
    }
  }
}

export default function FormsTest() {
  return (
    <>
      <Form method="post">
        <button type="submit">Post</button>
      </Form>
      <Form method="put">
        <button type="submit">Put</button>
      </Form>
      <Form method="patch">
        <button type="submit">Patch</button>
      </Form>
      <Form method="delete">
        <button type="submit">Delete</button>
```

```
    </Form>
    <Form method="get" action="/products">
      <input placeholder="Search products..." type="text" name="q" />
      <button type="submit">Search</button>
    </Form>
  </>
 );
}
```

This page has four <Form> elements with a different method set for each. Clicking on the submit button will log the method of the submitted form to the console. This demonstrates that we can handle multiple <Form> elements with differences in their method on a single page.

When clicking on the "Search" submit button belonging to the <Form> element with the method set to get, we are redirected to the /products URL assigned to the form's action property. The name and value of the form input are appended to the /products URL as search params.

The product creation route

Let's add a new route for the product creation page within the Router.tsx file. This route will have its path set to products/new within the child routes of the dashboard. We'll set the action of the route to point to the action function that we created above the DashboardNewProduct component.

```
import { createBrowserRouter } from "react-router-dom";
import Layout from "./components/Layout";
import DashboardLayout from "./components/DashboardLayout";
import ErrorPage from "./pages/Error";
import DashboardIndex from "./pages/dashboard/DashboardIndex";
import DashboardProducts, {
  loader as dashboardProductsLoader,
} from "./pages/dashboard/DashboardProducts";
import DashboardProduct, {
  loader as dashboardProductLoader,
} from "./pages/dashboard/DashboardProduct";
import DashboardNewProduct, {
  action as dashboardNewProductAction,
} from "./pages/dashboard/DashboardNewProduct";
//...

const router = createBrowserRouter([
  {
    path: "/",
    element: <Layout />,
```

```
      children: [
        //...
      ],
    },
    {
      path: "dashboard",
      element: <DashboardLayout />,
      children: [
        {
          errorElement: <ErrorPage />,
          children: [
            {
              index: true,
              element: <DashboardIndex />,
            },
            {
              path: "products",
              element: <DashboardProducts />,
              loader: dashboardProductsLoader,
            },
            {
              path: "products/:productId",
              element: <DashboardProduct />,
              loader: dashboardProductLoader,
            },
            {
              path: "products/new",
              element: <DashboardNewProduct />,
              action: dashboardNewProductAction,
            },
          ],
        },
      ],
    },
]);

export { router };
```

Now, when we click on the "Add New" button from the dashboard products page, we are taken to the product creation page.

Ranked route matching

The URL http://127.0.0.1:5173/products/new could technically be matched by two routes: products/new and products/:productId, where new could be the productId. However, we know that we want to load the first route for this URL, not the second one. The good news is that React Router knows this too.

When matching URLs to routes, React Router ranks routes according to the number of segments and picks the most specific match. This React Router feature is called ranked routes and removes any worry we might have about the ordering of our routes.

Product creation field validation

Besides adding the `required` attribute on the form `<input />` elements, we haven't added any form validation once the form is submitted.

We can validate form fields in the `action` function, and if we find validation errors, we can return error messages for the invalid fields in the `errors` object.

We will validate that the product `title` entered is more than one character long. Product titles are rarely one character in length. We will also validate that the `price` entered consists of digits, with a maximum of two decimal places permitted. Lastly, we will validate that the `imageUrl` entered is a valid URL. We'll introduce two validation helper functions, `isValidPrice` and `isValidUrl`, in a new `/src/utils/index.ts` file.

```
export function isValidPrice(price: string) {
  return price.match(/^\d+(\.\d{1,2})?$/);
}

export function isValidUrl(url: string) {
  try {
    new URL(url);
    return true;
  } catch (err) {
    return false;
  }
}
```

Next, let's add the form validation code in the `action` function with the help of these two helper functions.

For every invalid field, we will add the field name as a key to the `errors` object. The value of that key will be the error message. If the `errors` object has one or more keys within it after our validation checks are complete, we will return it to the component instead of moving ahead with product creation.

Lastly, if a form field has an error message, we will display it right below the form field. This only applies to the required fields. We won't need to do this for the product `description` field which is optional and has no validation rules.

```typescript
import { Form, redirect, useActionData } from 'react-router-dom';
import { addProduct } from '../../utils/fake-api';
import { isValidPrice, isValidUrl } from '../../utils';

export async function action({ request }: { request: Request }) {
  const errors: { [key: string]: string } = {};

  try {
    const formData = await request.formData();

    const title = formData.get('title') as string;
    const description = formData.get('description') as string;
    const price = formData.get('price') as string;
    const brand = formData.get('brand') as string;
    const category = formData.get('category') as string;
    const imageUrl = formData.get('imageUrl') as string;

    if (typeof title !== 'string' || title.length < 2) {
      errors.title = 'Product name must be more than one character.';
    } else if (!isValidPrice) {
      errors.price = 'Enter a valid price.';
    } else if (!isValidUrl(imageUrl)) {
      errors.imageUrl = 'Image URL must be a valid URL.';
    }

    if (Object.keys(errors).length) {
      return { errors };
    }

    await addProduct({
      title,
      description,
      price: parseFloat(price),
      brand,
      category,
      imageUrl,
    });

    return redirect(`/dashboard/products`);
  } catch (e) {
```

```
      errors.form = 'Product creation failed. Please try again later.';
      return { errors };
    }
}

export default function DashboardNewProduct() {
  const actionData = useActionData() as { errors: { [key: string]: string } }
;
  const { errors } = actionData ?? {};

  return (
    <div className="space-y-12">
      <header>
        <h1 className="font-bold text-3xl md:text-4xl">New Product</h1>
        <p className="text-lg">Create a new product.</p>
      </header>

      {errors?.form && <div className="bg-red-50 p-3 rounded text-red-800">{e
rrors?.form}</div>}

      <Form method="post" className="space-y-6">
        <label className="flex flex-col space-y-1">
          <span className="font-medium">Product title</span>
          <input type="text" name="title" required className="border p-2 roun
ded" />
          {errors?.title && <p className="text-red-800 text-sm">{errors.title
}</p>}
        </label>
        <label className="flex flex-col space-y-1">
          <span className="font-medium">Product description</span>
          <textarea name="description" className="border p-2 rounded" />
        </label>
        <label className="flex flex-col space-y-1">
          <span className="font-medium">Price</span>
          <input type="text" name="price" required className="border p-2 roun
ded" />
          {errors?.price && <p className="text-red-800 text-sm">{errors.price
}</p>}
        </label>
        <label className="flex flex-col space-y-1">
          <span className="font-medium">Brand</span>
          <input type="text" name="brand" required className="border p-2 roun
ded" />
          {errors?.brand && <p className="text-red-800 text-sm">{errors.brand
}</p>}
        </label>
        <label className="flex flex-col space-y-1">
          <span className="font-medium">Category</span>
          <input type="text" name="category" required className="border p-2 r
ounded" />
```

```
            {errors?.category && <p className="text-red-800 text-sm">{errors.ca
tegory}</p>}
        </label>
        <label className="flex flex-col space-y-1">
          <span className="font-medium">Image URL</span>
          <input type="text" name="imageUrl" required className="border p-2 r
ounded" />
          {errors?.imageUrl && <p className="text-red-800 text-sm">{errors.im
ageUrl}</p>}
        </label>
        <div>
          <button
            type="submit"
            className="bg-black hover:bg-gray-800 px-4 py-2 rounded text-whit
e"
          >
            Save
          </button>
        </div>
      </Form>
    </div>
  );
}
```

If the errors.title key exists, we display its value as an error message below the product title field. We do the same for all the other form fields and their corresponding keys in the errors object - except for the optional description field.

Adding products

Let's use the new product creation form to add a few products. You can add any products you want. Here is a list of products that I'll be adding.

```
title: "iPhone 14",
description: "The best smartphone by Apple.",
price: 599.99,
imageUrl: "https://i.dummyjson.com/data/products/1/thumbnail.jpg"
brand: "Apple",
category: "Smartphones",
---
title: "iPhone X",
description: "SIM-Free, Model A19211 6.5-inch Super Retina HD display with OL
ED technology A12 Bionic chip.",
price: 499.99,
imageUrl: "https://i.dummyjson.com/data/products/2/thumbnail.jpg"
brand: "Apple",
```

```
category: "Smartphones",
---
title: "Samsung Universe 9",
description: "Samsung's new variant which goes beyond Galaxy to the Universe.
",
price: 1249,
imageUrl: "https://i.dummyjson.com/data/products/3/thumbnail.jpg"
brand: "Samsung",
category: "Smartphones",
---
title: "OPPO F19",
description: "OPPO F19 is officially announced on April 2021.",
price: 280,
imageUrl: "https://i.dummyjson.com/data/products/4/thumbnail.jpg"
brand: "OPPO",
category: "Smartphones",
---
title: "Huawei P30",
description: "Huawei's re-badged P30 Pro New Edition.",
price: 499.99,
imageUrl: "https://i.dummyjson.com/data/products/5/thumbnail.jpg"
brand: "Huawei",
category: "Smartphones",
```

Editing products

Let's add the functionality to edit existing products. Create a new
/src/pages/dashboard/DashboardEditProduct.tsx file for the edit product page. In this file,
we'll create a new DashboardEditProduct page component.

We won't add a loader function to this file since we can reuse the loader function defined in
the DashboardProduct page component which loads a single product by its ID.

The edit product page component will contain the same form that we used for the product
creation page. The only difference will be that the form fields will be pre-populated with the data of the
product returned by our API for a given productId. Go ahead and copy the DashboardNewProduct
page component and paste it into the DashboardEditProduct page component.

The useLoaderData Hook in the DashboardEditProduct page component is used to
retrieve the product returned by the loader function. If product data is returned by the loader
function, we'll pre-populate the form fields using the defaultValue attribute on the elements. If not,
we'll redirect the user to the dashboard products page.

```jsx
import { Form, useLoaderData, useActionData, Navigate } from 'react-router-do
m';
import { siteConfig } from '../../config/site';
import { loader } from './DashboardProduct';

export default function DashboardEditProduct() {
  const product = useLoaderData() as Awaited<ReturnType<typeof loader>>;
  const actionData = useActionData() as { errors: { [key: string]: string } }
;
  const { errors } = actionData ?? {};

  if (!product) {
    return <Navigate to="/dashboard/products" replace={true} />;
  }

  return (
    <div className="space-y-12">
      <header>
        <h1 className="font-bold text-3xl md:text-4xl">Edit Product</h1>
        <p className="text-lg">Edit product details.</p>
      </header>

      {errors?.form && <div className="bg-red-50 p-3 rounded text-red-800">{e
rrors?.form}</div>}

      <Form method="post" className="space-y-6">
        <label className="flex flex-col space-y-1">
          <span className="font-medium">Product title</span>
          <input type="text" name="title" defaultValue={product.title} requir
ed className="border p-2 rounded" />
          {errors?.title && <p className="text-red-800 text-sm">{errors.title
}</p>}
        </label>
        <label className="flex flex-col space-y-1">
          <span className="font-medium">Product description</span>
          <textarea name="description" defaultValue={product.description} cla
ssName="border p-2 rounded" />
        </label>
        <label className="flex flex-col space-y-1">
          <span className="font-medium">Price</span>
          <input type="text" name="price" defaultValue={product.price} requir
ed className="border p-2 rounded" />
          {errors?.price && <p className="text-red-800 text-sm">{errors.price
}</p>}
        </label>
        <label className="flex flex-col space-y-1">
          <span className="font-medium">Brand</span>
          <input type="text" name="brand" defaultValue={product.brand} requir
ed className="border p-2 rounded" />
          {errors?.brand && <p className="text-red-800 text-sm">{errors.brand
```

```
}</p>}
        </label>
        <label className="flex flex-col space-y-1">
          <span className="font-medium">Category</span>
          <input type="text" name="category" defaultValue={product.category}
required className="border p-2 rounded" />
          {errors?.category && <p className="text-red-800 text-sm">{errors.ca
tegory}</p>}
        </label>
        <label className="flex flex-col space-y-1">
          <span className="font-medium">Image URL</span>
          <input type="text" name="imageUrl" defaultValue={product.imageUrl}
required className="border p-2 rounded" />
          {errors?.imageUrl && <p className="text-red-800 text-sm">{errors.im
ageUrl}</p>}
        </label>
        <div>
          <button
            type="submit"
            className="bg-black hover:bg-gray-800 px-4 py-2 rounded text-whit
e"
            disabled={isSubmitting}
          >
            Save
          </button>
        </div>
      </Form>
    </div>
  );
}
```

The DashboardEditProduct page component is using the useActionData Hook, which we
copied from the DashboardNewProduct page component. However, we have not defined an action
function for DashboardEditProduct yet. We'll do that next.

Editing a product

Let's create an action function above the DashboardEditProduct component. It will be
very similar to the action function that we used for the product creation form. The difference here is
that we'll be calling our API's editProduct function. We'll pass the function the productId URL
param as well as the validated data submitted by the form.

If the productId cannot be retrieved from the URL params in the action function, an error is
thrown.

```typescript
const path = 'dashboard/products/:productId/edit';

export async function action({
  request,
  params: { productId },
}: {
  request: Request;
  params: Params<ParamParseKey<typeof path>>;
}) {
  if (!productId) {
    throw new Error('Product not found.');
  }

  const errors: { [key: string]: string } = {};

  try {
    const formData = await request.formData();

    const title = formData.get('title') as string;
    const description = formData.get('description') as string;
    const price = formData.get('price') as string;
    const brand = formData.get('brand') as string;
    const category = formData.get('category') as string;
    const imageUrl = formData.get('imageUrl') as string;

    if (typeof title !== 'string' || title.length < 2) {
      errors.title = 'Product name must be more than one character.';
    } else if (!price.match(/^\d+(\.\d{1,2})?$/)) {
      errors.price = 'Enter a valid price.';
    } else if (!isValidUrl(imageUrl)) {
      errors.imageUrl = 'Image URL must be a valid URL.';
    }

    if (Object.keys(errors).length) {
      return { errors };
    }

    await editProduct(productId, {
      title,
      description,
      price: parseFloat(price),
      brand,
      category,
      imageUrl,
    });

    return redirect(`/dashboard/products`);
  } catch (e) {
    errors.form = 'Saving the product failed. Please try again later.';
    return { errors };
```

```
    }
}
```

You may have noticed that we are starting to encounter some redundancy in our code. There is some redundant logic in the `action` functions of both the `DashboardNewProduct` and `DashboardEditProduct` components. We could move this redundant logic to helper functions stored in a new file that would sit in the `utils` folder.

Also, both the `DashboardNewProduct` and `DashboardEditProduct` components have redundant forms. We could extract the form to a new `ProductForm` component that gets reused in both components. We could also create an `Error` component to display form errors, replacing the redundant code to display errors. We'll leave these optimizations out since we want to focus on React Router's features.

Edit product route

Let's create a dynamic route for the edit product page within `Router.tsx` file.

We'll add a route with a `products/:productId/edit` path within the child routes of the dashboard. We'll set this route's `element` to the `DashboardEditProduct` page component that we just created. We'll set the route's `loader` property to the same `loader` function used on the `products/:productId` route. Lastly, we'll set the route's `action` property to the `action` function that we created above the `DashboardEditProduct` page component.

```tsx
import { createBrowserRouter } from "react-router-dom";
import Layout from "./components/Layout";
import ErrorPage from "./pages/Error";
import DashboardLayout from "./components/DashboardLayout";
import DashboardIndex from "./pages/dashboard/DashboardIndex";
import DashboardProducts, {
  loader as dashboardProductsLoader,
} from "./pages/dashboard/DashboardProducts";
import DashboardNewProduct, {
  action as dashboardNewProductAction,
} from "./pages/dashboard/DashboardNewProduct";
import DashboardProduct, {
  loader as dashboardProductLoader,
} from "./pages/dashboard/DashboardProduct";
import DashboardEditProduct, {
  action as dashboardEditProductAction,
} from "./pages/dashboard/DashboardEditProduct";
```

```
//...

const router = createBrowserRouter([
  {
    path: "/",
    element: <Layout />,
    children: [
      //...
    ],
  },
  {
    path: "dashboard",
    element: <DashboardLayout />,
    children: [
      {
        errorElement: <ErrorPage />,
        children: [
          {
            index: true,
            element: <DashboardIndex />,
          },
          {
            path: "products",
            element: <DashboardProducts />,
            loader: dashboardProductsLoader,
          },
          {
            path: "products/:productId",
            element: <DashboardProduct />,
            loader: dashboardProductLoader,
          },
          {
            path: "products/new",
            element: <DashboardNewProduct />,
            action: dashboardNewProductAction,
          },
          {
            path: "products/:productId/edit",
            element: <DashboardEditProduct />,
            loader: dashboardProductLoader,
            action: dashboardEditProductAction,
          },
        ],
      },
    ],
  },
]);

export { router };
```

Edit and delete buttons

Let's add "Edit" and "Delete" buttons to the single product page (the `DashboardProduct` page component). We'll add the buttons just below the product details. These buttons will allow us to edit and delete products without having to know the direct URL to do so.

For the "Edit" button, we'll add a submit button within a `<Form>` with an `action` set to `edit`. For the "Delete" button, we'll add a submit button within another `<Form>` with an `action` set to `destroy`.

```
import { Form, ParamParseKey, Params, useLoaderData } from 'react-router-dom';
import { siteConfig } from '../../config/site';
import { Product } from '../../types';

const path = 'dashboard/products/:productId';

export async function loader({ params: { productId } }: { params: Params<ParamParseKey<typeof path>> }) : Promise<Product | null> {
  if (productId) {
    return getProduct(productId);
  }

  return null;
}

export default function DashboardProduct() {
  const product = useLoaderData() as Awaited<ReturnType<typeof loader>>;

  if (!product) {
    return <Navigate to="/dashboard/products" replace={true} />;
  }

  return (
    <div className="space-y-12">
      <header className="space-y-2">
        <h1 className="font-bold text-3xl md:text-4xl">{product.title}</h1>
        <p className="text-lg">{product.description}</p>
      </header>
      <aside>
        <img src={product.imageUrl} />
      </aside>
      <section>
        <dl className="space-y-4">
          <div>
```

```
                <dt className="font-medium">Brand</dt>
                <dd>{product.brand}</dd>
              </div>
              <div>
                <dt className="font-medium">Category</dt>
                <dd>{product.category}</dd>
              </div>
              <div>
                <dt className="font-medium">Price</dt>
                <dd>{product.price}</dd>
              </div>
            </dl>
          </section>
          <section className="flex items-center space-x-2">
            <Form action="edit">
              <button type="submit" className="bg-black hover:bg-gray-800 px-4 py
-2 rounded text-white">
                Edit
              </button>
            </Form>
            <Form
              method="post"
              action="destroy"
              onSubmit={(event) => {
                if (!confirm('Are you sure you want to delete this product?')) {
                  event.preventDefault();
                }
              }}
            >
              <button type="submit" className="bg-red-500 hover:bg-red-600 px-4 p
y-2 rounded text-white">
                Delete
              </button>
            </Form>
          </section>
        </div>
      );
    }
```

Since both of the <Form> elements are rendered in the dashboard/products/:productId route, they will apply the action of the form relative to the current route.

The <Form> with an action set to destroy will submit the form to dashboard/products/:productId/destroy when the "Delete" button is clicked. The <Form> with an action set to edit will submit the form to dashboard/products/:productId/edit when the "Edit" button is clicked. In both cases, the :productId represents the id of the current product being viewed.

When the "Delete" button is clicked, we will prompt the user for a delete confirmation to make sure that they did not accidentally hit the button. If the user does not provide a delete confirmation, we prevent the submit event from going forward. Next, let's implement the deletion of products.

Deleting products

Let's create a new DashboardDestroyProduct page component within a new /src/pages/dashboard/DashboardDestroyProduct.tsx file. Within this file, we'll add an action function that will be used for the product destroy route (dashboard/products/:productId/destroy).

The action function will receive the productId from the URL params and pass it to the deleteProduct function of our API. If no productId is found, an error is thrown.

```
import { ParamParseKey, Params, redirect } from "react-router-dom";
import { deleteProduct } from "../../utils/fake-api";

const path = "dashboard/products/:productId/delete";

export async function action({
  params: { productId },
}: {
  params: Params<ParamParseKey<typeof path>>,
}) {
  if (!productId) {
    throw new Error("Product not found.");
  }

  await deleteProduct(productId);

  return redirect(`/dashboard/products`);
}
```

Product deletion route

Let's add a new product deletion route within the dashboard routes. This route will have its path set to products/:productId/destroy within the child routes of the dashboard. This route will also have its action set to the action function that we created in DashboardDestroyProduct.

```
import { createBrowserRouter } from "react-router-dom";
import Layout from "./components/Layout";
```

```
import DashboardLayout from "./components/DashboardLayout";
import ErrorPage from "./pages/Error";
import { action as destroyAction } from "./pages/dashboard/DashboardDestroyPr
oduct";
//...

const router = createBrowserRouter([
  {
    path: "/",
    element: <Layout />,
    children: [
      //...
    ],
  },
  {
    path: "dashboard",
    element: <DashboardLayout />,
    children: [
      {
        errorElement: <ErrorPage />,
        children: [
          //...
          {
            path: "products/:productId/destroy",
            action: destroyAction,
          },
        ],
      },
    ],
  },
]);

export { router };
```

Let's visit the dashboard products page and clicking on a product in the list. We'll be taken to the single product page, where we can now choose to edit or delete the product by clicking on the corresponding button.

If we click on the "Delete" button and confirm our deletion in the deletion prompt, the product will be deleted. Clicking on the "Edit" button takes us to the edit product form where we can make changes to the product details. The changes are saved and we are taken back to the dashboard products page.

Browsing products

The product pages that we created in the previous section were for the store administrator(s) to manage their products within the dashboard. In an upcoming section of the book, we'll secure the dashboard pages with authentication and authorization, allowing only signed-in users with the right privileges to access the dashboard.

In this section, we'll focus on setting up the public product pages that will allow customers to browse the store. We'll also add interactive elements to the store, such as:

- Styling active links in the main menu.
- Adding a loading indicator during navigation.
- Handling the "submitting" state of forms.

Public product pages

Let's create the public product pages so that users can browse the products offered by our store.

Products page

Copy the `DashboardProducts` page component and paste it into a new `/src/pages/Products.tsx` file, where we will define a new `Products` component.

Remove the "Add New" button and modify the page heading and subheading. We will not define a new `loader` function for this page since we can reuse the same `loader` from the `DashboardProducts` page component.

```
import { useLoaderData } from 'react-router-dom';
import ProductsList from '../components/ProductsList';
import { loader } from './dashboard/DashboardProducts';

export default function Products() {
  const { products } = useLoaderData() as Awaited<ReturnType<typeof loader>>;

  return (
    <div className="space-y-12">
```

```
      <header>
        <div>
          <h1 className="font-bold text-3xl md:text-4xl">Shop Products</h1>
          <p className="text-lg">Shop our products.</p>
        </div>
      </header>
      <section>
        <ProductsList products={products} />
      </section>
    </div>
  );
}
```

One issue here is that `ProductCard` component, used to render products within the `ProductsList` component, has its links set to the dashboard product page rather than the public product page.

We could introduce a `productUrl` prop in `ProductCard` to solve this issue. However, we'd also have to add a `productUrl` prop to `ProductsList` so that it can forward it to `ProductCard`. This is starting to dig us into a *prop drilling* hole. A better solution is to use *component composition*.

Let's create a `Card` component as well as sub-components for the various sections of a card that we want to support, such as `CardImage`, `CardTitle`, etc. This will provide us with lots of flexibility on how we build and display cards across our app. Depending on the page that a `Card` is rendered on (public page or dashboard page), we'll be able to set the right URL for the card image and the card title.

```
import { ReactNode } from "react";

type Props = {
  children: ReactNode,
  className?: string,
};

export function Card({ children }: Props) {
  return (
    <div className="border rounded-lg p-3 space-y-4 shadow-lg">{children}</di
v>
  );
}

export function CardImage({ children }: Props) {
  return <div className="relative aspect-square">{children}</div>;
}

export function CardContent({ children }: Props) {
```

```
    return <div className="space-y-2">{children}</div>;
}

export function CardTitle({ children }: Props) {
  return <h3 className="text-lg font-medium">{children}</h3>;
}

export function CardDescription({ children }: Props) {
  return <p className="text-sm text-gray-600">{children}</p>;
}
```

Now, let's update the `Products` component to make use of the new composable `Card` component and its sub-components that we just created. This will allow us to use the public product page URL for the card image and the card title.

```
import { useLoaderData } from 'react-router-dom';
import ProductsList from '../components/ProductsList';
import { loader } from './dashboard/DashboardProducts';
import { Card, CardContent, CardDescription, CardImage, CardTitle } from '../
components/Card';

export default function Products() {
  const { products } = useLoaderData() as Awaited<ReturnType<typeof loader>>;

  return (
    <div className="space-y-12">
      <header>
        <div>
          <h1 className="font-bold text-3xl md:text-4xl">Shop Products</h1>
          <p className="text-lg">Shop our products.</p>
        </div>
      </header>
      <section>
        {products.length ? (
          <div className="grid grid-cols-1 lg:grid-cols-3 gap-6">
            {products.map((product) => (
              <Card key={product.id}>
                <CardImage>
                  <Link to={`/products/${product.id}`}>
                    <img src={product.imageUrl} className="object-cover aspec
t-square rounded-t-lg" />
                  </Link>
                </CardImage>
                <CardContent>
                  <CardTitle>
                    <Link to={`/products/${product.id}`}>{product.title}</Lin
k>
                  </CardTitle>
```

```
                <CardDescription>{product.description}</CardDescription>
              </CardContent>
            </Card>
          ))}
        </div>
      ) : (
        <p className="bg-gray-50 border text-gray-500 p-6 rounded-lg">No pr
oducts found.</p>
      )}
    </section>
  </div>
);
}
```

We can also update the DashboardProducts component to use our new Card component, but this time, using the dashboard product page URL for the image and title links. Thanks to the flexibility that we achieved with the Card component and its sub-components, we no longer need the ProductList and ProductCard components. We can delete them.

Single product page

Copy the DashboardProduct page component and paste it into a new /src/pages/SingleProduct.tsx file, where we will define a new SingleProduct component. We purposely avoided naming the page Product because it would clash with the Product type that we created.

Remove the "Edit" and "Delete" buttons and reuse the same loader function from the DashboardProduct page component.

```
import { useLoaderData, Navigate } from 'react-router-dom';
import { loader } from './dashboard/DashboardProduct';

export default function SingleProduct() {
  const product = useLoaderData() as Awaited<ReturnType<typeof loader>>;

  if (!product) {
    return <Navigate to="/products" replace={true} />;
  }

  return (
    <div className="space-y-12">
      <header className="space-y-2">
        <h1 className="font-bold text-3xl md:text-4xl">{product.title}</h1>
        <p className="text-lg">{product.description}</p>
```

```
    </header>
    <aside>
      <img src={product.imageUrl} />
    </aside>
    <section>
      <dl className="space-y-4">
        <div>
          <dt className="font-medium">Brand</dt>
          <dd>{product.brand}</dd>
        </div>
        <div>
          <dt className="font-medium">Category</dt>
          <dd>{product.category}</dd>
        </div>
        <div>
          <dt className="font-medium">Price</dt>
          <dd>{product.price}</dd>
        </div>
      </dl>
    </section>
  </div>
 );
}
```

Routes for product pages

Let's create new routes in `Router.tsx` for the public product pages that we created above. The products page's `path` will simply be set to `products`, while the single product page's `path` will be set to `products/:productId`.

Let's take opportunity to nest all the public routes within a pathless route with its `errorElement` set to `ErrorPage`. This way, if an error occurs in any of these routes, particularly in the product-related pages, the custom `ErrorPage` will be displayed.

We'll nest this pathless route within the root route so that it will be displayed within the app's Layout when an error occurs in the public pages. Then, we'll nest all public routes within the children of this pathless route.

```
import { createBrowserRouter } from "react-router-dom";
import Home from "./pages/Home";
import About from "./pages/About";
import NotFound from "./pages/NotFound";
import Layout from "./components/Layout";
import ErrorPage from "./pages/Error";
import Products from "./pages/Products";
```

```
import SingleProduct from "./pages/SingleProduct";
import DashboardLayout from "./components/DashboardLayout";
import DashboardProducts, {
  loader as dashboardProductsLoader,
} from "./pages/dashboard/DashboardProducts";
import DashboardProduct, {
  loader as dashboardProductLoader,
} from "./pages/dashboard/DashboardProduct";
//...

const router = createBrowserRouter([
  {
    path: "/",
    element: <Layout />,
    children: [
      {
        errorElement: <ErrorPage />,
        children: [
          {
            index: true,
            element: <Home />,
          },
          {
            path: "about",
            element: <About />,
          },
          {
            path: "products",
            element: <Products />,
            loader: dashboardProductsLoader,
          },
          {
            path: "products/:productId",
            element: <SingleProduct />,
            loader: dashboardProductLoader,
          },
          {
            path: "*",
            element: <NotFound />,
          },
        ],
      },
    ],
  },
  {
    path: "dashboard",
    element: <DashboardLayout />,
    children: [
      {
        errorElement: <ErrorPage />,
```

```
      children: [
        //...
      ],
    },
  ],
},
]);

export { router };
```

When we navigate to `http://127.0.0.1:5173/products`, we see a products page that is similar to the one we created within the dashboard.

Clicking on an individual product in the list takes us to `http://127.0.0.1:5173/products/:productId`, where `:productId` is the `id` of the product that we clicked on. A single product page, similar to the one we created within the dashboard, is displayed.

Styling active links

Let's add a link to the new products page from the main menu. We will now use React Router's `<NavLink>` component instead of the `<Link>` component for the main menu links.

A `<NavLink>` is a special kind of `<Link>` that knows whether or not it is an "active" link. This allows us to show which menu link is currently selected by styling it differently. We could also add additional information for assistive technology such as screen readers.

When the user navigates to the URL specified in the `<NavLink>`, its `isActive` property will be `true`. This allows us to use CSS to style it differently from the other non-active links.

When a `<NavLink>` is about to be active (the data is still loading), an `isPending` property will be `true`. This is helpful if we want to provide immediate feedback on links that have been clicked but are not fully loaded yet.

```
import { Link, NavLink } from "react-router-dom";
import { siteConfig } from "../config/site";

export default function Header() {
  const getNavLinkClasses = ({ isActive }: { isActive: boolean }) => {
    return isActive ? "font-semibold" : "";
  };
```

```
    return (
      <header className="sticky w-full border-b shadow-sm backdrop-blur">
        <div className="container flex items-center h-14 mx-auto">
          <div className="flex items-center space-x-6 md:gap-10">
            <Link to="/">
              <h1 className="font-bold">{siteConfig.name}</h1>
            </Link>
            <nav className="flex items-center space-x-6">
              <NavLink to="/about" className={getNavLinkClasses}>
                About
              </NavLink>
              <NavLink to="/products" className={getNavLinkClasses}>
                Products
              </NavLink>
            </nav>
          </div>
        </div>
      </header>
    );
}
```

We created a getNavLinkClasses method that checks the isActive property on a
<NavLink>. If isActive is true, then the text within the link will get a bolder styling so that it
appears emphasized.

Navigation loading state

As users navigate the app, React Router will leave the old page up as data is still loading for the
next page. This can make the app feel a little unresponsive as we click between products in the list of
products. We can provide the user with feedback so that navigating the app doesn't feel unresponsive.

React Router has a useNavigation Hook that returns the current navigation state. The
navigation state that it returns can be "idle", "submitting", or "loading".

There are several different ways that we can represent the loading state. We can lower the
opacity of the content, show a spinner, or show a loading bar across the top.

Let's add the useNavigation Hook in the Layout component. Then, let's check if the
navigation state is in a "loading" state. If it is, we'll lower the opacity of the element that wraps the
Outlet. This will make the page content appear faded until loading is complete.

```
import { Outlet, useNavigation } from "react-router-dom";
import Footer from "./Footer";
import Header from "./Header";
import TopBarProgress from "react-topbar-progress-indicator";

export default function Layout() {
  const navigation = useNavigation();
  const isLoading = navigation.state === "loading";

  return (
    <main className="flex flex-col min-h-screen">
      <Header />
      <div
        className={`container mx-auto py--24 ${
          navigation.state === "loading" ? "opacity-25" : ""
        }`}
      >
        <Outlet />
      </div>
      <Footer />
    </main>
  );
}
```

We can also add a loading progress indicator at the top of the app. For this, we'll use the

react-topbar-progress-indicator package. Let's install it.

```
yarn add react-topbar-progress-indicator
```

Next, let's import the package, configure the loading progress bar colors, and display the

<TopBarProgress /> component when the navigation is in a "loading" state.

```
import { Outlet, useNavigation } from "react-router-dom";
import Footer from "./Footer";
import Header from "./Header";
import TopBarProgress from "react-topbar-progress-indicator";

TopBarProgress.config({
  barColors: {
    0: "#fff",
    "1.0": "#000",
  },
  shadowBlur: 0,
});

export default function Layout() {
  const navigation = useNavigation();
  const isLoading = navigation.state === "loading";
```

```
  return (
    <main className="flex flex-col min-h-screen">
      {isLoading && <TopBarProgress />}
      <Header />
      <div
        className={`container mx-auto py-24 ${isLoading ? "opacity-25" : ""}`
}
      >
        <Outlet />
      </div>
      <Footer />
    </main>
  );
}
```

If we navigate to the public products page, or if we click on a product from the list of products, we'll notice a loading progress bar indicator displayed very briefly at the top of the app. We'll also notice that the content is initially displayed with a lower opacity, until the page is fully loaded. These convenient indicators inform the user that the app is currently in a "loading" state.

We can add the same loading indicators to the DashboardLayout component so that the store administrators will also be able to know when the app is in a "loading" state.

Form "submitting" state

The useNavigation Hook can also helps us detect a "submitting" state. The useNavigation Hook will return a "submitting" state whenever a route action is triggered by the submission of a form.

If we detect a "submitting" state, we can disable the form submit buttons so that the user cannot submit the form multiple times while one submission is still pending.

Let's use the useNavigation Hook within the DashboardNewProduct, DashboardEditProduct, DashboardProduct components. Then, let's define an isSubmitting variable that will be true when the navigation state is "submitting".

```
import { useNavigation } from "react-router-dom";

//...

const navigation = useNavigation();
const isSubmitting = navigation.state === "submitting";
```

Let's add the `disabled` property to the submit buttons in the DashboardNewProduct and DashboardEditProduct page components. This will disable the submit buttons while the form is submitting.

```
<button
  type="submit"
  className="bg-black hover:bg-gray-800 px-4 py-2 rounded text-white"
  disabled={isSubmitting}
>
  Save
</button>
```

Let's also add the `disabled` property to the submit buttons in the DashboardProduct page component. Both submit buttons will be disabled while one of the forms is still submitting.

```
<section className="flex items-center space-x-2">
  <Form action="edit">
    <button
      type="submit"
      className="bg-black hover:bg-gray-800 px-4 py-2 rounded text-white"
      disabled={isSubmitting}
    >
      Edit
    </button>
  </Form>
  <Form
    method="post"
    action="destroy"
    onSubmit={(event) => {
      if (!confirm("Are you sure you want to delete this product?")) {
        event.preventDefault();
      }
    }}
  >
    <button
      type="submit"
      className="bg-red-500 hover:bg-red-600 px-4 py-2 rounded text-white"
      disabled={isSubmitting}
    >
      Delete
    </button>
  </Form>
</section>
```

Product interactions

In this section, we'll add more advanced product interactions to our public product pages, such as:

- Searching for products.

- Adding a product to a wish list.

Searching for products

Let's modify the Products page to allow users to search for products. We'll introduce a new loader function for the Products page rather than relying on the loader from the DashboardProducts page component. This new loader function will read a search parameter q from the URL. We'll pass the search parameter to the getProducts function from our API. The getProducts function filters the list of products when a search term is present. If not, it simply returns the entire list of products.

Then, we'll add a React Router Form with an input field for the search term. When the text in the input field changes, it will call an onChange function that programatically submits the form rather than relying on the user to click a submit button.

```
import { Form, Link, useLoaderData, useSubmit } from 'react-router-dom';
import { ChangeEvent } from 'react';
import { Card, CardContent, CardDescription, CardImage, CardTitle } from '../
components/Card';
import { Product } from '../types';
import { getProducts } from '../utils/fake-api';

export async function loader({ request }: { request: Request }) : Promise<{ p
roducts: Product[]; q: string }> {
  const url = new URL(request.url);
  const q = url.searchParams.get('q') ?? '';

  const products = await getProducts(q);

  return { products, q };
}

export default function Products() {
  const { products, q } = useLoaderData() as Awaited<ReturnType<typeof loader
>>;
```

```
const submit = useSubmit();

const onChange = (e: ChangeEvent<HTMLInputElement>) => {
  // if search term is present, replace current entry in history stack
  const isFirstSearch = !q.length;
  submit(e.currentTarget.form, {
    replace: !isFirstSearch,
  });
};

return (
  <div className="space-y-12">
    <header>
      <div>
        <h1 className="font-bold text-3xl md:text-4xl">Shop Products</h1>
        <p className="text-lg">Shop our products.</p>
      </div>
    </header>
    <section>
      <Form role="search" className="flex items-center space-x-4">
        <input
          placeholder="Search products..."
          type="search"
          name="q"
          defaultValue={q}
          onChange={onChange}
          className="border outline-none p-2 rounded w-full md:w-1/4"
        />
      </Form>
    </section>
    <section>
      {products.length ? (
        <div className="grid grid-cols-1 lg:grid-cols-3 gap-6">
          {products.map((product) => (
            <Card key={product.id}>
              <CardImage>
                <Link to={`/products/${product.id}`}>
                  <img src={product.imageUrl} className="object-cover aspec
t-square rounded-t-lg" />
                </Link>
              </CardImage>
              <CardContent>
                <CardTitle>
                  <Link to={`/products/${product.id}`}>{product.title}</Lin
k>
                </CardTitle>
                <CardDescription>{product.description}</CardDescription>
              </CardContent>
            </Card>
          ))}
```

```
        </div>
      ) : (
        <p className="bg-gray-50 border text-gray--500 p-6 rounded-lg">No pr
oducts found.</p>
      )}
    </section>
  </div>
);
}
```

The first argument to submit is the form to be submitted. The second argument is a set of options for the form submission. We set replace to true when the search term is present. This will replace the current entry in the browser's history stack instead of creating a new one.

We are staying on the same /products page even as we're searching for products. Therefore, there's no need to create a new entry in the browser's history stack for every new search term. It would just end up spamming the browser's history stack with search terms.

Search route loader

Let's change the loader that we configured on the products route in Router.tsx. Remove dashboardProductsLoader as the loader. Instead, add the new loader that we just created above the Products page component.

```
import Products, { loader as productsLoader } from "./pages/Products";

//...

{
  path: 'products',
  element: <Products />,
  loader: productsLoader,
},
```

Search loading indicator

Let's add a loading indicator while the user's search request is still loading. This will inform the user of the progress of their search.

Let's use the useNavigation Hook to check for a search loading state. We'll check the navigation.location object for this.

The `navigation.location` object is present when the app navigates to a new URL and loads the data for it. It then goes away when there is no pending navigation anymore. Our app navigates to a new URL and loads the data for it every time `submit` is triggered, which is on every change to the search input.

When the search is in a loading state, we'll make the search input read-only (so that the user can't submit a new search) and we'll show a loading spinner beside the search input. We'll use an `<svg />` element from Flowbite (https://flowbite.com/docs/components/spinner/) to create the loading spinner.

```
import { Form, Link, useLoaderData, useNavigation, useSubmit } from 'react-ro
uter-dom';
import { ChangeEvent } from 'react';
import { Card, CardContent, CardDescription, CardImage, CardTitle } from '../
components/Card';
import { Product } from '../types';
import { getProducts } from '../utils/fake-api';

export async function loader({ request }: { request: Request }): Promise<{ pr
oducts: Product[]; q: string }> {
  const url = new URL(request.url);
  const q = url.searchParams.get('q') ?? '';

  const products = await getProducts(q);

  return { products, q };
}

export default function Products() {
  const { products, q } = useLoaderData() as Awaited<ReturnType<typeof loader
>>;
  const submit = useSubmit();
  const navigation = useNavigation();

  const isLoading = navigation.location && new URLSearchParams(navigation.loc
ation.search).has('q');

  const onChange = (e: ChangeEvent<HTMLInputElement>) => {
    // if search term is present, replace current entry in history stack
    const isFirstSearch = !q.length;
    submit(e.currentTarget.form, {
      replace: !isFirstSearch,
    });
  };

  return (
```

```
<div className="space-y-12">
  <header>
    <div>
      <h1 className="font-bold text-3xl md:text-4xl">Shop Products</h1>
      <p className="text-lg">Shop our products.</p>
    </div>
  </header>
  <section>
    <Form role="search" className="flex items-center space-x-4">
      <input
        placeholder="Search products..."
        type="search"
        id="q"
        name="q"
        defaultValue={q}
        onChange={onChange}
        readOnly={isLoading}
        className="border outline-none p-2 rounded w-full md:w-1/4"
      />
      <div className={isLoading ? '' : 'hidden'}>
        <svg
          aria-hidden="true"
          className="w-8 h-8 mr-2 text-gray-200 animate-spin fill-black"
          viewBox="0 0 100 101"
          fill="none"
          xmlns="http://www.w3.org/2000/svg"
        >
          <path
            d="M100 50.5908C100 78.2051 77.6142 100.591 50 100.591C22.385
8 100.591 0 78.2051 0 50.5908C0 22.9766 22.3858 0.59082 50 0.59082C77.6142 0.
59082 100 22.9766 100 50.5908ZM9.08144 50.5908C9.08144 73.1895 27.4013 91.509
4 50 91.5094C72.5987 91.5094 90.9186 73.1895 90.9186 50.5908C90.9186 27.9921
72.5987 9.67226 50 9.67226C27.4013 9.67226 9.08144 27.9921 9.08144 50.5908Z"
            fill="currentColor"
          />
          <path
            d="M93.9676 39.0409C96.393 38.4038 97.8624 35.9116 97.0079 33
.5539C95.2932 28.8227 92.871 24.3692 89.8167 20.348C85.8452 15.1192 80.8826 1
0.7238 75.2124 7.41289C69.5422 4.10194 63.2754 1.94025 56.7698 1.05124C51.766
6 0.367541 46.6976 0.446843 41.7345 1.27873C39.2613 1.69328 37.813 4.19778 38
.4501 6.62326C39.0873 9.04874 41.5694 10.4717 44.0505 10.1071C47.8511 9.54855
51.7191 9.52689 55.5402 10.0491C60.8642 10.7766 65.9928 12.5457 70.6331 15.25
52C75.2735 17.9648 79.3347 21.5619 82.5849 25.841C84.9175 28.9121 86.7997 32.
2913 88.1811 35.8758C89.083 38.2158 91.5421 39.6781 93.9676 39.0409Z"
            fill="currentFill"
          />
        </svg>
        <span className="sr-only">Loading...</span>
      </div>
    </Form>
```

```
        </section>
        <section>
          {products.length ? (
            <div className="grid grid-cols-1 lg:grid-cols-3 gap-6">
              {products.map((product) => (
                <Card key={product.id}>
                  <CardImage>
                    <Link to={`/products/${product.id}`}>
                      <img src={product.imageUrl} className="object-cover aspec
t-square rounded-t-lg" />
                    </Link>
                  </CardImage>
                  <CardContent>
                    <CardTitle>
                      <Link to={`/products/${product.id}`}>{product.title}</Lin
k>
                    </CardTitle>
                    <CardDescription>{product.description}</CardDescription>
                  </CardContent>
                </Card>
              ))}
            </div>
          ) : (
            <p className="bg-gray-50 border text-gray-500 p-6 rounded-lg">No pr
oducts found.</p>
          )}
        </section>
      </div>
  );
}
```

Debouncing the search

One serious limitation with the current search is that it updates the URL on every keystroke change in the search input. This can become a performance bottleneck since a request to the API endpoint is sent every time the URL is updated. Making so many network requests for a user's search is not efficient.

We can improve the performance of search by adding a debounce function. We'll set the debounce function to only update the URL in intervals of 500 milliseconds. This results in a very small delay in the display of search results as users type their search term, but it's an important performance improvement for our app.

We'll use the lodash debounce (https://lodash.com/docs/4.17.15#debounce) function to achieve this. First, install lodash and its corresponding types.

```
yarn add lodash
yarn add -D @types/lodash
```

Let's update the onChange event handler function in the Products page component to make use of the debounce function.

```
const onChange = useCallback(
  debounce((form: HTMLFormElement | null) => {
    // if search term is present, replace current entry in history stack
    const isFirstSearch = !q.length;
    submit(form, {
      replace: !isFirstSearch,
    });
  }, 500),
  [q] // function will only be created once (initially)
);
```

We wrapped the debounce function with the useCallback Hook to cache it between re-renders. This means that the debounce function will only be created once, during the initial component render, and not re-created on every component render. Re-creating the debounce function on every component render is not necessary and can become computationally expensive, so it's best to avoid it.

We will need to update the onChange property on the search input. Rather than just forwarding the ChangeEvent that occurs to the onChange event handler function, we will only pass a reference to the form that triggered the event.

```
onChange={(e) => onChange(e.currentTarget.form)}
```

We made this modification because e.currentTarget.form will always be null within the debounce function, giving us the following error when we try searching.

```
Uncaught TypeError: Cannot read properties of null (reading 'form')
```

Now, when we try searching for a product, the search feels more realistic. There is a 500-millisecond delay between when we type in a search term and when search results are displayed. This allows the search to be conducted with more characters from the user's search term. This approach to searching is more effective than the previous approach, where we conducted a new search for every single new character typed.

Clearing the search term

If we try searching for a product (ex: "iPhone") and then click on the browser back button, we'll notice that the search term has been cleared from the URL. However, the stale search term is still being displayed in the search input. The `loader` function also executes when navigating back in the browser. Thus, the list of products displayed is no longer being filtered by the stale search term. However, the stale search term that's still in the search input is misleading to users.

We need to synchronize the search input with the latest value being returned by the `loader` function, even when navigating back in the browser. When navigating back, the `loader` function still runs and returns a search term that is an empty string.

Let's add a React `useEffect` Hook to listen for changes on the search term returned by the `loader` function. Then, we can manipulate the state of the search input directly in the DOM, bypassing React's virtual DOM.

```
useEffect(() => {
  const input: HTMLInputElement | null = document.getElementById('q') as HTML
InputElement | null;
  if (input) {
    input.value = q;
  }
}, [q]);
```

We retrieve the value of the search input by its `id`. If a valid `HTMLInputElement` object is returned, then we set its value to the latest value of q, the search term.

We could have used React's `useState` Hook to manage the state of the search term. This would have made the `Products` component a *controlled* component. However, we actually don't control the URL, the user does with their browser's back and forward buttons. Therefore, we can simply manipulate the DOM to ensure that the search input reflects the latest state of the URL.

Wishlist

We've seen forms that change data but also cause some sort of navigation to happen. For example, `<Form action="edit" />` navigated to an `/products/:productId/edit` route and `<Form action="destroy" />` navigated to a `/products/:productId/destroy` route.

Sometimes, we need to change data with a form, but not change page. For such cases, we can use React Router's <Form /> without an action property, or we can use React Router's useFetcher Hook.

All the loader functions we interacted with so far depended on navigation to a certain route. Sometimes, we may want to call a loader function outside of navigation. Or, we may want to call an action function without any URL changes. We may want to interact with the server apart from navigation events. The useFetcher Hook connects a component's UI directly to action and loader functions without navigating.

Let's add a wishlist button on the public single product page. The user will be able to click the button to add or remove a product from their wishlist. The React Router useFetcher Hook is a good solution for this because we simply want to change the product's isInWishlist property on the current page that we're on, without changing pages.

Rather than using React Router's <Form /> element that we've been using, we can use <fetcher.Form />, made available to us by the useFetcher Hook. It works almost the same as <Form />. If we give it a method of post, it will call the action function and then reload all the data for the route. The only difference that <fetcher.Form /> has with an element like <Form action="edit"> is that it doesn't make any URL changes. It leaves the browser history stack unaffected.

```
import { Navigate, ParamParseKey, Params, useFetcher, useLoaderData } from 'r
eact-router-dom';
import { loader } from './dashboard/DashboardProduct';
import { editProduct } from '../utils/fake-api';

const path = 'products/:productId';

export async function action({
  request,
  params: { productId },
}: {
  request: Request;
  params: Params<ParamParseKey<typeof path>>;
}) {
  if (!productId) {
    throw new Error('Product not found.');
  }

  try {
```

```
    const formData = await request.formData();

    const isInWishlist = formData.get('wishlist') === 'true';

    return editProduct(productId, { isInWishlist });
  } catch (e) {
    const error = 'An error occurred. Please try again later.';
    return { error };
  }
}

export default function SingleProduct() {
  const product = useLoaderData() as Awaited<ReturnType<typeof loader>>;
  const fetcher = useFetcher();

  if (!product) {
    return <Navigate to="/products" replace={true} />;
  }

  const isSubmitting = fetcher.state === 'loading';
  const isInWishlist = product.isInWishlist;

  return (
    <div className="space-y-12">
      <header className="space-y-2">
        <h1 className="font-bold text-3xl md:text-4xl">{product.title}</h1>
        <p className="text-lg">{product.description}</p>
      </header>
      <aside>
        <img src={product.imageUrl} />
      </aside>
      <section>
        <dl className="space-y-4">
          <div>
            <dt className="font-medium">Brand</dt>
            <dd>{product.brand}</dd>
          </div>
          <div>
            <dt className="font-medium">Category</dt>
            <dd>{product.category}</dd>
          </div>
          <div>
            <dt className="font-medium">Price</dt>
            <dd>{product.price}</dd>
          </div>
        </dl>
      </section>
      <section className="space-y-6">
        <fetcher.Form method="post">
          <button
```

```
              name="wishlist"
              type="submit"
              value={isInWishlist ? 'false' : 'true'}
              className="bg-black hover:bg-gray-800 px-4 py-2 rounded text-whit
e"
              disabled={isSubmitting}
          >
              {isInWishlist ? 'Remove from Wishlist' : 'Add to Wishlist'}
          </button>
        </fetcher.Form>
      </section>
    </div>
  );
}
```

We referenced the `fetcher.state` to check the `useFetcher` loading state. If we are in a
"loading" state, we disable the wishlist button to avoid sending more than one request at a time.

We toggle the button label based on whether the current product is in the wishlist or not. We
also toggle the button value to `true` if the current product is in the wishlist, and `false` if it is not. We
added a `name` prop with a value of `wishlist` to the button so that it behaves like a form field. As a
result, the submitted form's `formData` will contain a `wishlist` key that will either be `true` or `false`.

Since `<fetcher.Form />` has its `method` set to `post`, it will call the `action` function. We
added an `action` function that retrieves the form data from the request and calls the `editProduct`
function from our API, passing along the value of the `wishlist` field. The API's `editProduct` function
will be responsible for saving the product's wishlist state in the `isInWishlist` field.

If an error occurs in the `action` function, an error object is returned. The error message can be
displayed by referencing `fetcher.data.error`.

Wishlist route action

Let's configure the `action` property on the single product route by assigning to it the `action`
function that we just added above the `SingleProduct` component.

```
import SingleProduct, {
  action as singleProductAction,
} from "./pages/SingleProduct";

//...
```

```
<Route
  path="/products/:productId"
  element={<SingleProduct />}
  loader={dashboardProductLoader}
  action={singleProductAction}
/>;
```

We can now try clicking on the "Add to wishlist" button. After the milliseconds of artificial API delay are up, you'll notice that the button is now displayed as a "Remove from wishlist" button. This means that the product is now in the user's wishlist. If we click the button again, the button is once again displayed as an "Add to wishlist" button. This means that the product has been removed from the user's wishlist.

Wishlist action errors

Let's simulate an error in the wishlist action function by adding throw new Error() as the first line in the try block. We won't see any difference because we are not yet handling the error. Let's handle the error.

Let's use the react-toastify package to show form submission errors with a toast notification when fetcher.data.error is defined. First, install the package.

```
yarn add react-toastify
```

Next, let's add a ToastContainer in the Layout component so that we don't have to re-define the container for toast notifications on every single page. Let's also import the default stylesheet that react-toastify provides us with to style the toasts.

```
//...
import { ToastContainer } from 'react-toastify';
import "react-toastify/dist/ReactToastify.css";

//...

export default function Layout() {
  //...

  return (
    <main className="flex flex-col min-h-screen">
      {isLoading && <TopBarProgress />}
      <Header />
      <div
        className={`container mx-auto py-24 ${isLoading ? "opacity-25" : ""}`
```

```
    }
        >
          <Outlet />
        </div>
        <Footer />
        <ToastContainer />
      </main>
    );
}
```

Next, let's trigger the toast.error function when fetcher.data.error is defined. We'll pass the error message returned by fetcher.data.error into the toast notification. We'll set a toastId for this error to prevent duplicate toast notifications from being displayed.

```
import { toast } from 'react-toastify';
//...

export default function SingleProduct() {
  //...

  const notify = () => toast.error(fetcher.data?.error, { toastId: 'error' })
;

  if (fetcher.data?.error) {
    notify();
  }

  return (
    //...
  )
}
```

Now, let's try again to simulate an error in the action function. Be sure to add throw new Error() as the first line in the try block of the action function. We now see a temporary toast error notification displayed at the top right of the screen. The toast contains the error message returned by the action function, "An error occurred. Please try again later." We can choose to manually close the toast or wait for it to automatically disappear.

Optimistic UI strategy

You may have noticed that the app felt somewhat unresponsive when we clicked on the "Add to wishlist" button. This was due to the artificial network latency that we added to our fake API. There will be real latency in the real world, so it was important to simulate it.

To give the user who clicked the button some feedback while they are waiting for the network request to complete, we can use the "optimistic UI" strategy.

The "optimistic UI" strategy simulates the results of a data mutation by updating the UI even before receiving a response from the server.

We can retrieve the form data submitted to the `action` function via the `fetcher.formData` property. We can then use this data to immediately update the button's state - even though the network request hasn't completed yet.

You might be wondering, what if the network request fails. No problem. When it does fail, the UI will revert back to the actual data returned by the `loader` function for the current product.

Let's change the `isInWishlist` variable declaration to use `let` so that we can re-assign a value to `isInWishlist`. If the `fetcher.formData` property is present and no error is returned by the `action` function, we will assign the value of the `wishlist` key in `fetcher.formData` to the `isInWishlist` variable. This will override its default value returned by the `loader` function (`product.isInWishlist`).

```
let isInWishlist = product.isInWishlist;
if (fetcher.formData && !fetcher.data?.error) {
  isInWishlist = fetcher.formData.get("wishlist") === "true";
}
```

Now, clicking on the wishlist button feels much more responsive! The wishlist feature is a bit unrealistic because it allows any user, even those not signed-in, to be able to add products to their wishlist. In the next section, we'll add authentication to our app so that we can limit the wishlist feature to signed-in users only.

Authentication

In this section, we'll add authentication to our app. One of the easiest ways to add authentication to a new React app is to use Clerk (https://clerk.com).

Clerk provides complete user authentication and user management via its APIs and pre-built React components. Clerk is purpose-built for React. Clerk's goal is to handle user management so that developers don't have to keep re-inventing the wheel when it comes to adding authentication to their apps.

After adding authentication to our app, we'll also add authorization. This will limit dashboard access to only those users who have an "Admin" role.

Installing Clerk

Let's install Clerk into our project using the following command.

```
yarn add @clerk/clerk-react
```

Next, create a `.env.local` file in the root of our project. We'll need it to set the Clerk publishable key as an environment variable.

The Clerk publishable key is available to us from the **API Keys** menu option in the **Developers** menu. Clerk allows you to select *Development* or *Production* as an environment, both of which provide different keys. We'll use the Development key for this exercise.

Your `.env.local` file should now look like the following.

```
VITE_REACT_APP_CLERK_PUBLISHABLE_KEY=pk_test_...
```

Vite loads the `.env.local` file in all cases. This file is automatically ignored by Git so that you don't accidentally commit secure keys to a GitHub repository. If you want to commit your Vite environment variables to your GitHub repository, you can use an `.env` file instead or remove the `*.local` line in the `.gitignore` file.

Setting up Clerk

Clerk requires our React application to be wrapped in the `<ClerkProvider/>` component. The `<ClerkProvider />` component provides active session and user context to Clerk's Hooks and other components.

In `main.tsx`, create a `ClerkProviderLayout` component that serves as the `<ClerkProvider />` route wrapper, rendering an `Outlet` slot so that it can render child routes within it.

```
const ClerkProviderLayout = () => {
  const navigate = useNavigate();

  if (!import.meta.env.VITE_REACT_APP_CLERK_PUBLISHABLE_KEY) {
    throw new Error("Missing Publishable Key");
  }

  const clerkPubKey = import.meta.env.VITE_REACT_APP_CLERK_PUBLISHABLE_KEY;

  return (
    <ClerkProvider publishableKey={clerkPubKey} navigate={(to) => navigate(to
)}>
      <Outlet />
    </ClerkProvider>
  );
};
```

Vite exposes environment variables on the special `import.meta.env` object, allowing us to reference our Clerk publishable key. If no such key is found, an error is thrown.

Router update

Next, let's convert the object-based routes in `Router.tsx` to component-based routes, using the React Router `<Route />` component. This will make it easier to merge our existing routes within the `ClerkProvider` and to use the helpful components that Clerk provides us with.

Clerk provides us with ready-made `SignIn` and `SignUp` components that we can use as our login and registration pages.

Clerk also provides us with `SignedIn` and `SignedOut` components that we can use to configure what our dashboard pages should display, depending on whether the user is signed-in or not. When the user is signed-in, the dashboard pages should render. When the user is signed out, and they try to access a dashboard page, they should be redirected to the sign-in page. This can easily be achieved with the Clerk `RedirectToSignIn` component.

```
const router = createBrowserRouter(
  createRoutesFromElements(
    <Route element={<ClerkProviderLayout />}>
      <Route path="/" element={<Layout />}>
        <Route errorElement={<ErrorPage />}>
          <Route index element={<Home />} />
          <Route path="/about" element={<About />} />
          <Route path="/products" element={<Products />} loader={productsLoad
er} />
          <Route path="/products/:productId" element={<SingleProduct />} load
er={dashboardProductLoader} />
          <Route path="/sign-in/*" element={<SignIn routing="path" path="/sig
n-in" />} />
          <Route path="/sign-up/*" element={<SignUp routing="path" path="/sig
n-up" />} />
          <Route path="*" element={<NotFound />} />
        </Route>
      </Route>
      <Route path="/dashboard">
        <Route
          element={
            <>
              <SignedIn>
                <DashboardLayout />
              </SignedIn>
              <SignedOut>
                <RedirectToSignIn />
              </SignedOut>
            </>
          }
        >
          <Route errorElement={<ErrorPage />}>
            <Route index element={<DashboardIndex />} />
            <Route path="products" loader={dashboardProductsLoader} element={
<DashboardProducts />} />
            <Route path="products/new" action={dashboardNewProductAction} ele
ment={<DashboardNewProduct />} />
            <Route path="products/:productId" loader={dashboardProductLoader}
element={<DashboardProduct />} />
            <Route
              path="products/:productId/edit"
```

```
            loader={dashboardProductLoader}
            action={dashboardEditProductAction}
            element={<DashboardEditProduct />}
          />
          <Route path="products/:productId/destroy" action={dashboardDestro
yProductAction} />
        </Route>
      </Route>
    </Route>,
  ),
);

ReactDOM.createRoot(document.getElementById('root') as HTMLElement).render(
  <React.StrictMode>
    <RouterProvider router={router} />
  </React.StrictMode>,
);
```

With our new Clerk-powered router in place, we can go ahead and delete the previous

Router.tsx file that we were using since we aren't using it anymore.

Authentication redirects

Let's configure our authentication redirects within Clerk. Sign in to your Clerk account and

complete the following steps.

Sign-in redirect
- Click the **Paths** menu option in the **Developers** menu.
- Go to the **Sign-in** section
- In the text box for **After sign-in redirect**, enter /dashboard.

Sign-up redirect
- Click the **Paths** menu option in the **Developers** menu.
- Go to the **Sign-up** section
- In the text box for **After sign-up redirect**, enter /dashboard.

Sign-out redirect
- Click the **Paths** menu option in the **Developers** menu.
- Go to the **Sign-out** section
- In the text box for **Sign-out redirect, all accounts**, enter /sign-in.

Now, when we sign in or sign up, our app will automatically redirect us to the /dashboard page. When we sign out, our app will automatically redirect us to the /sign-in page.

Sign-in and sign-out links

Let's update the Header component to include sign-in and sign-out links, depending on whether the user is already signed-in or not. For this, we can use the useUser Hook provided by Clerk. It makes an isSignedIn boolean variable available to us.

If the user is not signed-in, we will show a sign-in link. If the user is signed-in, we will show a link to the dashboard. We will also render the <UserButton /> component provided by Clerk. This component shows a user avatar that can be clicked on. When clicked on, a popup menu is displayed with options to manage one's user account or to sign out.

```
import { Link, NavLink } from "react-router-dom";
import { siteConfig } from "../config";
import { useUser, UserButton } from "@clerk/clerk-react";

export default function Header() {
  const { isSignedIn } = useUser();

  const getNavLinkClasses = ({ isActive }: { isActive: boolean }) => {
    return isActive ? "font-semibold" : "";
  };

  return (
    <header className="sticky w-full border-b shadow-sm backdrop-blur">
      <div className="container flex items-center justify-between h-14 mx-auto">
        <div className="flex items-center space-x-6 md:gap-10">
          <Link to="/">
            <h1 className="font-bold">{siteConfig.name}</h1>
          </Link>
          <nav className="flex items-center space-x-6">
            <NavLink to="/about" className={getNavLinkClasses}>
              About
            </NavLink>
            <NavLink to="/products" className={getNavLinkClasses}>
              Products
            </NavLink>
          </nav>
        </div>
        {isSignedIn && (
          <div className="flex items-center space-x-4">
```

```
          <UserButton />
          <NavLink to="/dashboard" className={getNavLinkClasses}>
            Dashboard
          </NavLink>
        </div>
      )}
      {!isSignedIn && (
        <div className="flex items-center space-x-4">
          <NavLink to="/sign-in" className={getNavLinkClasses}>
            Sign in
          </NavLink>
        </div>
      )}
    </div>
  </header>
);
}
```

Click on the sign-in link to try signing in to our app with the email that you used for Clerk. You should be redirected to the /dashboard page. If you sign out, you should be redirected to the /sign-in page. If you are signed out and try accessing the /dashboard page, you will be asked to sign in.

Authorization

Let's add *authorization* to our app so that only users with an *admin* role can access the dashboard area. Users without the *admin* role are just regular customers of our store, so we don't want them accessing our store's administrative dashboard.

Sign in to your Clerk account and click on the **Organizations** menu option.

1.   Create an organization called "Staff".

2.   Select your email address as the owner of the organization.

3.   Add yourself as a member of the organization with the role "Admin".

Next, let's create a useAdmin custom Hook within our app. It will be responsible for checking if the signed-in user has a role of "Admin". Create this Hook in a new /src/hooks/useAdmin.ts file.

```
import { useUser } from "@clerk/clerk-react";

export default function useAdmin() {
  const { isLoaded, isSignedIn, user } = useUser();

  if (!isLoaded || !isSignedIn) {
```

```
    return null;
  }

  return user.organizationMemberships.some((item) => item.role === "admin");
}
```

Next, in main.tsx, create an AdminAuthorization component that makes use of the useAdmin Hook. If the useAdmin Hook does not return true, the user is not an "Admin". As a result, the AdminAuthorization component will redirect the user to a 404 page.

```
function AdminAuthorization({ children }: { children: ReactNode }) {
  const navigate = useNavigate();
  const isAdmin = useAdmin();

  useEffect(() => {
    if (!isAdmin) {
      navigate(`/404`);
    }
  }, [isAdmin, navigate]);

  return children;
}
```

Next, wrap the <DashboardLayout /> component with the new AdminAuthorization component that we just created.

```
<>
  <SignedIn>
    <AdminAuthorization>
      <DashboardLayout />
    </AdminAuthorization>
  </SignedIn>
  <SignedOut>
    <RedirectToSignIn />
  </SignedOut>
</>
```

Lastly, let's update the Header component so that the link to the dashboard is only displayed if the user has a role of "Admin".

```
import { Link, NavLink } from "react-router-dom";
import { siteConfig } from "../config";
import { useUser, UserButton } from "@clerk/clerk-react";
import useAdmin from "../hooks/useAdmin";

export default function Header() {
  const { isSignedIn } = useUser();
```

```
  const isAdmin = useAdmin();

  const getNavLinkClasses = ({ isActive }: { isActive: boolean }) => {
    return isActive ? "font-semibold" : "";
  };

  return (
    <header className="sticky w-full border-b shadow-sm backdrop-blur">
      <div className="container flex items-center justify-between h-14 mx-aut
o">
        <div className="flex items-center space-x-6 md:gap-10">
          <Link to="/">
            <h1 className="font-bold">{siteConfig.name}</h1>
          </Link>
          <nav className="flex items-center space-x-6">
            <NavLink to="/about" className={getNavLinkClasses}>
              About
            </NavLink>
            <NavLink to="/products" className={getNavLinkClasses}>
              Products
            </NavLink>
          </nav>
        </div>
        {isSignedIn && (
          <div className="flex items-center space-x-4">
            <UserButton />
            {isAdmin && (
              <NavLink to="/dashboard" className={getNavLinkClasses}>
                Dashboard
              </NavLink>
            )}
          </div>
        )}
        {!isSignedIn && (
          <div className="flex items-center space-x-4">
            <NavLink to="/sign-in" className={getNavLinkClasses}>
              Sign in
            </NavLink>
          </div>
        )}
      </div>
    </header>
  );
}
```

If a user signs in and does not have a role of "Admin" associated to them within Clerk, they will be taken to a 404 page. The site header will only display Clerk's `<UserButton />` but not a link to the dashboard, which is meant for store administrators.

An idea here is that we could introduce a new customer dashboard area for non-admin users, perhaps using a /customer path. They could be redirected there when they sign in. We would simply have to change the URL that the AdminAuthorization component redirects users to when they don't have an "Admin" role. It would change from /404 to /customer. We could then update the Header component to show a link to the customer dashboard if the user is signed in but is not an administrator.

Wishlist for signed-in users

Now that we have authentication set up in our app, we can make the wishlist button more realistic by restricting it to signed-in users only. If a user is not signed-in and they click on the wishlist button, they should be redirected to the sign-in page. We'll use Clerk's useUser Hook to retrieve the user's isSignedIn state.

We can assign isSignedIn to a hidden input in the fetcher.Form.

```
<input type="hidden" name="isSignedIn" value={`${isSignedIn}`} />
```

Then, before calling editProduct in the action function, we can redirect the user to the sign-in page if they are not signed-in.

```
import { redirect } from "react-router-dom";

//...

if (formData.get("isSignedIn") !== "true") {
  return redirect(`/sign-in`);
}
```

Can we do better that this approach? Yes we can. We don't even have to submit the form if the user is not signed-in. We can add an onClick property to the wishlist button and assign an event handler function to it. In this event handler function, we can check if the isSignedIn value from the useUser Hook is true. If it's not true, we prevent the default form submission behavior and redirect the user to the sign-in page with the help of the useNavigate Hook. If isSignedIn is true, then the default form submission behavior proceeds uninterrupted.

Here is the SingleProduct component with the latest changes applied to it.

```
import { Navigate, ParamParseKey, Params, redirect, useFetcher, useLoaderData
, useNavigate } from 'react-router-dom';
```

```
import { loader } from './dashboard/DashboardProduct';
import { editProduct } from '../utils/fake-api';
import { useUser } from '@clerk/clerk-react';
import { toast } from 'react-toastify';
import { MouseEvent } from 'react';

const path = 'products/:productId';

export async function action({
  request,
  params: { productId },
}: {
  request: Request;
  params: Params<ParamParseKey<typeof path>>;
}) {
  if (!productId) {
    throw new Error('Product not found.');
  }

  try {
    const formData = await request.formData();

    if (formData.get('isSignedIn') !== 'true') {
      return redirect(`/sign-in`);
    }

    const isInWishlist = formData.get('wishlist') === 'true';

    return editProduct(productId, { isInWishlist });
  } catch (e) {
    const error = 'An error occurred. Please try again later.';
    return { error };
  }
}

export default function SingleProduct() {
  const product = useLoaderData() as Awaited<ReturnType<typeof loader>>;
  const { isSignedIn } = useUser();
  const fetcher = useFetcher();
  const navigate = useNavigate();

  if (!product) {
    return <Navigate to="/products" replace={true} />;
  }

  const isSubmitting = fetcher.state === 'loading';
  let isInWishlist = product.isInWishlist;
  if (fetcher.formData && !fetcher.data?.error) {
    isInWishlist = fetcher.formData.get('wishlist') === 'true';
  }
```

```
  const notify = () => toast.error(fetcher.data?.error, { toastId: 'error' })
;

  if (fetcher.data?.error) {
    notify();
  }

  const onClick = (e: MouseEvent<HTMLButtonElement>) => {
    if (!isSignedIn) {
      e.preventDefault();
      navigate('/sign-in');
    }
  };

  return (
    <div className="space-y-12">
      <header className="space-y-2">
        <h1 className="font-bold text-3xl md:text-4xl">{product.title}</h1>
        <p className="text-lg">{product.description}</p>
      </header>
      <aside>
        <img src={product.imageUrl} />
      </aside>
      <section>
        <dl className="space-y-4">
          <div>
            <dt className="font-medium">Brand</dt>
            <dd>{product.brand}</dd>
          </div>
          <div>
            <dt className="font-medium">Category</dt>
            <dd>{product.category}</dd>
          </div>
          <div>
            <dt className="font-medium">Price</dt>
            <dd>{product.price}</dd>
          </div>
        </dl>
      </section>
      <section className="space-y-6">
        <fetcher.Form method="post">
          <input type="hidden" name="isSignedIn" value={`${isSignedIn}`} />
          <button
            name="wishlist"
            type="submit"
            value={isInWishlist ? 'false' : 'true'}
            className="bg-black hover:bg-gray-800 px-4 py-2 rounded text-whit
e"

            disabled={isSubmitting}
```

```
            onClick={onClick}
          >
            {isInWishlist ? 'Remove from Wishlist' : 'Add to Wishlist'}
          </button>
        </fetcher.Form>
      </section>
    </div>
  );
}
```

What's next?

Congratulations on completing this book! You've gained a solid understanding of how to build modern web applications with React, React Router, and TypeScript.

Throughout this book, we've explored the core concepts of React Router version 6.14+. We also learned how to build a realistic app with React Router from start to finish. Let's summarize the topics that we've covered in this book.

- How to create basic routes and dynamic routes.
- How to create nested routes.
- How to use multiple layouts in a single app.
- How to build forms with React Router.
- How to handle route errors and routes that are not found.
- How to style active links.
- How to handle form and navigation loading states.
- How to create a performant search.
- How to add authentication and authorization with Clerk.
- How to create a protected section of the app.
- How to use actions and loaders to create, view, update, and delete products.
- How to interact with an API layer for data creation, mutation, and deletion requests.
- How to connect a UI directly to actions and loaders without navigating.
- How to add TailwindCSS classes to style a React app with React Router.
- How to set up a new project with Vite, React, TypeScript, React Router, and more.
- How to configure Prettier and ESLint with Vite.

By mastering the fundamentals of the most popular routing library for React, React Router, there is no limit to what you can build next!

If you haven't already, I invite you to read my book on the fundamentals of React, React Ready (https://lumin8media.com/books/react-ready-learn-modern-react-with-typescript), to become an even more skilled and confident React developer.

I hope you enjoyed your journey through this book. I invite you to visit my website (https://lumin8media.com) for more JavaScript, TypeScript, and React content to help you continue your learning journey.

If you're looking for a next topic to learn, I would suggest learning how to use one or both of the two popular full stack React frameworks with server-side rendering, Remix and Next.js.

Remix

Remix (https://remix.run) is a popular full stack React framework that provides server-side rendering. It was created by the creators of React Router. Remix is built on top of React Router, which means that most of what we learned in this book can be applied to Remix.

Next.js

Next.js (https://nextjs.org) is another popular full stack React framework that provides server-side rendering. Next.js version 13 introduced a new App Router (https://nextjs.org/docs/app/building-your-application) with new features and conventions that differ from its origina pages router (https://nextjs.org/docs/pages/building-your-application). The App Router supports one of React's latest features, Server Components.

Upgrading to Next.js 13 does not require using the new App Router. Next.js 13 can still be used with the pages router. If you're just getting started with Next.js, I would suggest learning it with the App Router.